JEREMY NAYDLER
theology and religious studies, and is a philosopher, cultural
historian and gardener who lives and works in Oxford,
England. He has long been interested in the history of
consciousness and sees the study of past cultures—which
were more open to the world of spirit than our own, pre-
dominantly secular, culture—as relevant both to understanding our situation
today and to finding pathways into the future. His longstanding concern
about the impact of electronic technologies on our inner life and on our
relationship to nature has found expression in his book *In the Shadow of the
Machine* (Temple Lodge 2018) and in numerous articles contributed to mag-
azines such as *New View, Self and Society* and *Resurgence*.

Praise for *In The Shadow of the Machine*:

'*A brilliant and penetrating study of the prehistory of the computer in relation to the
evolution of consciousness... His book is a spiritual beacon reminding us that our
essence transcends the material and the mechanical.*' – David Lorimer, *Paradigm
Explorer*

'*A marvellous and erudite account of the history of consciousness... The range and
depth of Naydler's investigation is vast. He identifies and brings out the significance
of key, often little-remarked changes in thinking... [and] offers new, insightful perspectives.*' – Richard Gault, *Beshara Magazine*

'*This important and profoundly thought-provoking book is a must-read for anyone
with an itch in the back of their mind that something is very wrong with the world
today. [It] takes us on the fascinating journey of the human mind from the very dawn
of time to today, the age of the computer. In doing so, we are forced to question the
very nature of our reality...*' – Brett Lothian, *New Dawn*

'*This mportant book illuminates contemporary consciousness powerfully, and offers
a crucial exploration of what it means to be human.*' – Mark Vernon, *author of
A Secret History of Chrisitanity*

'*Jeremy Naydler has become, in my judgement, one of the most interesting and original living writers in Britain.*' – Professor Bruce G. Charlton, *author of Addicted
to Distraction*

OTHER BOOKS BY JEREMY NAYDLER:

Goethe on Science (1996)

Temple of the Cosmos: The Ancient Egyptian Experience of the Sacred (1996)

Shamanic Wisdom in the Pyramid Texts: The Mystical Tradition of Ancient Egypt (2005)

Soul Gardening (2006)

The Future of the Ancient World: Essays on the History of Consciousness (2009)

Gardening as a Sacred Art (2011)

In the Shadow of the Machine, The Prehistory of the Computer and the Evolution of Consciousness (2018)

THE STRUGGLE FOR A HUMAN FUTURE

5G, AUGMENTED REALITY AND THE INTERNET OF THINGS

JEREMY NAYDLER

TEMPLE LODGE

Temple Lodge Publishing Ltd.
Hillside House, The Square
Forest Row, RH18 5ES

www.templelodge.com

Published by Temple Lodge 2020

A CIP catalogue record for this book is available from the British Library

ISBN 9781912230433

Cover by Morgan Creative featuring 'The Archangel Michael Struggles with Satan' by
William Blake
Typeset by Symbiosys Technologies, Visakhapatnam, India
Printed and bound by 4Edge Ltd., Essex

Contents

INTRODUCTION

Remembering the Totality of Who We Are

The Digital Revolution has a way of constantly running ahead of its commentators. As it keeps taking novel forms and dazzling us with devices that have new and greater capabilities, we find that whatever technologies are in vogue today are all too soon superseded by newer, more powerful and even more seductive technologies tomorrow. This Proteus-like character of the Digital Revolution is part of its nature, but underlying its changing outer forms, there are deeper and more constant currents moving beneath the surface. It is these currents that are the real driving forces of the Digital Revolution, but they are more hidden than the latest smartwatch, headset or digital assistant.

The five essays gathered together in this book are concerned especially with the nature of these more hidden driving forces that stand behind the unfolding Digital Revolution. The latest phase of this revolution involves (amongst other things) the rollout of 5G, the establishment of the Internet of Things, the creation of a so-called 'smart planet' and the growing use by human beings of Augmented Reality and Virtual Reality technologies. These developments are, however, symptomatic of a deeper process to which we should attend. For while each new technological innovation or upgrade promises many benefits, they come at a certain cost, which is borne both by the human soul and by the natural environment in which we live.

In the Western wisdom tradition, there is a recurrent theme of humanity's self-forgetfulness. We find it, for example, in Plato, in the *Corpus Hermeticum*, in Boethius's *The Consolation of Philosophy* and in Gnostic texts such as the *Hymn of the Pearl*, to which we shall turn in Chapter Two. This self-forgetfulness is a forgetting of our spiritual origins, and of the fact that human nature has a transcendent source. The person we ordinarily identify with is not the totality of who we are. This totality includes a spiritual kernel of which we are for the most part unconscious, and yet is nevertheless the foundation of our being, and our relationship to it is the secret of true happiness.

The wisdom traditions of both West and East have perennially sought to inculcate awareness of this spiritual kernel, in order to counteract the tendency of humans of all cultural epochs to forget and to neglect our spiritual origins. Where we today differ from cultures of the past is that not only do we suffer from the forgetfulness that is part of the human condition, but we also pay scant attention to the wisdom traditions that seek to rouse us to remembrance. Instead, the whole thrust of contemporary culture is towards distraction, fragmentation and dispersion of consciousness. The Digital Revolution has carried this tendency to an extreme, so much so that if we had deliberately set out to design technologies to induce the distractedness and self-forgetfulness that traditional spirituality has always endeavoured to save us from, then we could hardly have done better. This in turn has led to many of us failing to notice just how corrosive these developments can be to the essential human task of remembering the totality of who we are.

But as well as inducing distractedness and self-forgetfulness, our technologies are the vehicles of something else, potentially far more detrimental to our wellbeing.

The Inhuman

Towards the end of his life, the post-modernist thinker Jean-François Lyotard formulated a question that haunts the times we live in. It lurks beneath the surface of our consciousness, for most of us unarticulated and for that reason all the more menacing. Lyotard had the sensitivity to understand its profound importance, and hence the need to raise it to conscious awareness. The question that he formulated is this:

> What if what is 'proper' to humankind were to be inhabited by the inhuman? [1]

By the 'inhuman' we should understand that which is essentially hostile to the human. Lyotard distinguished two kinds of 'inhuman'—one is the inhumanity of our social, political and economic systems. The other is the 'infinitely secret' inhumanity that invades the soul and holds it hostage.[2] It is this latter kind of inhumanity that is the more insidious of the two, and it is this that, as our relationship with our digital devices becomes ever more intimate, poses the greatest danger to us. For the inhuman is carried towards us by our technologies. While we can stand back from and critique the inhumanity of the social, political and economic systems in which we live, our personal susceptibility to the ingress of the inhuman puts us in far greater jeopardy. This susceptibility has been exploited by the direction that our digital technologies have taken, which has been unwaveringly towards accommodating themselves within the sphere of the human. As they have evolved, they have adapted themselves to the human body as well as to the human soul, becoming physically smaller and lighter and at the same time more powerful and capable.

The first computers were so large we had to stand in front of them or walk around them in order to operate them. With the invention of desktop computers it became possible to sit in front of them and engage with them, as it were, face to face. Then it became possible to put computers in our pocket, and now it is possible, with smartwatches and smartglasses, to wear them. At each stage the interface between them and us has become more 'human friendly', while at the same time humans have inwardly adjusted to relating to them on a day-to-day, hour-by-hour and even minute-by-minute basis. So while the computer has been moulding itself to the contours of the human body and soul, the inner life of human beings has slowly but surely been moulded towards a greater degree of computer-compatibility—affecting our language, our thought-processes and our daily habits. In this evolving symbiosis, in which we have become ever more intertwined with the computer, we have also become more dependent on it. Biological integration is not far away. It is the logical next step. It is of utmost importance, therefore, that we open our eyes to the fact that even though human beings are the inventors, manufacturers and eager consumers of digital technologies, the driving force behind the Digital Revolution is not simply human: the 'inhuman' is also seeking to be realized within the human.

But how are we to characterize this spectre of the inhuman? Human beings have always had the tendency to fall away from their essential nature. For pre-industrial humanity, the danger was conceived in terms of our descending to the animal or bestial level, captives of our untransformed instinctual drives and passions. That, we could say, is to fall beneath the human level: to fall into the sub-human. In our industrial and post-industrial age, the primary danger to our humanity lies less in succumbing to instincts and passions than in succumbing to the cold inhumanity of the machine and the unfeeling, compassionless algorithm. That is to fall into the inhuman. Both tendencies live within us, and both work to undermine the possibility of realizing our true human potential, but today it is the peril of the inhuman that we must especially guard against. Its aim is to totally supplant the human, and it will surely succeed, should we fail to ground ourselves in the authentically human. We must wake up to the prospect of the colonization of the human by the inhuman and, in full awareness of the gravity of the threat posed by the inhuman, consciously take on the challenge of living humanly.

To Live Humanly

What does it mean to live humanly? If the totality of who we are includes a spiritual kernel of which we are for the most part unconscious, then it follows that to live humanly must be to live in greater consciousness of it. It is incumbent on us to strengthen our sense that this spiritual kernel is our deepest and truest self, and therefore the part of us with which we should seek to identify. This requires that we engage in the arduous work of inner transformation, so that those desires, inclinations and deep-seated habits of thought, which draw us away from that essential remembrance, are slowly changed, and become inwardly aligned with what the wisdom traditions tell us is the true centre of our being. This moral effort of turning towards, and rooting ourselves in, the spiritual kernel of who we are also involves a shift in the quality of our thinking. This shift is from reliance on a result-oriented, discursive thinking that runs along from one thought to another, towards giving more value to the stillness and open receptivity of the act of contemplation. Boethius gives the beautiful image of the seekers of truth having to bend their wandering consciousness into a circle, and teach their souls 'to lodge in the treasure house' at its centre. For there they will find a light, stronger even than the light of the sun, which will illumine their minds from within.[3]

This 'contemplative turn' has always been regarded as the foundation of the spiritual life, but it is of especial relevance to us today. Our technologies are based on the automation of logical analysis, calculation and problem solving, and are fundamentally discursive and result-oriented: they are hyperactive and aim always to output results. By contrast, the act of contemplation brings the mind to a standstill: it is not result-oriented, it cannot be automated, and it can only be engaged for its own sake. It enables us to gain insights into the deeper meaning of things, about which machine thinking knows nothing. These insights can well up from the imaginal world as powerful archetypal images, for contemplative thinking borders on imaginative vision. But equally they can take the form of ideas or intuitions that, like rays of light, illumine a question or life situation from a more comprehensive standpoint. Contemplation is often described as involving the opening of an inner eye of the soul. It is referred to as 'the mind's eye' or 'the eye of the heart', and through it we become aware of what is invisible to the physical eye.[4] This more interior source of knowing, which is unconditioned by habits of thought and opinion, could also be described as entailing an opening of the 'inner ear' of the soul to the voice of conscience. It can guide us towards a sense of moral certainty about what it is we should or should not do, and to the ideals that can inspire our actions.

Aristotle maintained that an action is only fully our own when we have 'carried back the origin of the action' to this contemplative part of ourselves, referred to as the *nous*, or 'the centre of spiritual intelligence' within a person.[5] Once it has been carried back to this source, then the action is entirely free because it has been chosen from the centre, rather than from the periphery, of ourselves. In the Western wisdom tradition, the defining characteristic of any action that is truly human is that it is free, precisely because it stems from this originating source. In Aristotle, Thomas Aquinas and Rudolf Steiner, we find this vital tenet reiterated: that we cannot adequately conceive of what it means to live humanly if we exclude freedom. Freedom belongs to the essence of human nature.[6] That is not to say we necessarily live from the essence of ourselves every moment of the day. Far from it! But the trouble is that our digital technologies, because of their tendency to scatter the soul, don't help us to do this. Rather they introduce a dark undertow with which we must constantly contend, if we are to carry back the origin of our actions to the centre of ourselves.

This movement back to the centre is the premise of true freedom. It is not given to us on a plate: it has to be won. To become free, we must engage in the work of inner transformation previously referred to, which involves permeating the everyday self and its fantasies, obsessions and desires with the clearly conceived aims that spring from the inmost source of who we are. In Christian mysticism this inner work is called *theosis*, or 'making divine'.[7] Another word used to describe it was coined by the Italian poet Dante, who called this inner work 'to transhumanize' (*trasumanare*).[8] The verb 'to transhumanize' well expresses the fact that our core human striving must be to overcome ourselves, so that we go beyond the 'merely human' life lived at the periphery of who we are. It is a sign of our times that today 'Transhumanism' is a materialistic ideology that seeks to technologically 'enhance' the human being. Contemporary Transhumanists fail to grasp that to go beyond the merely human can only be achieved by grounding ourselves in the transcendent, and this requires dedicated soul-work, sustained by the spiritual discipline of coming back to the still point at the centre of the circle.

As one of the most influential ideologies steering the Digital Revolution, the contemporary Transhumanist movement shows us the price that the Digital Revolution threatens to exact from us. The price is that we lose our ability to know the meaning and purpose of the spiritual life, we lose even our ability to understand the language that the wisdom traditions use. And ultimately we lose our humanity as, overcome by the collective amnesia regarding what it means to realize our deeper human potential, we succumb to the inhuman.

The Interiority of Nature

From nature, too, a price is exacted by the Digital Revolution, which has swamped the natural environment with a complex mix of artificially generated electromagnetic fields. As a result, not just human beings but all living organisms are exposed to levels of electromagnetic radiation far in excess of natural background levels.[9] It would be unwise to assume that this does not have any adverse effect on the wellbeing of living organisms and the ecosystems to which they belong. A growing number of studies show that many organisms are highly sensitive to electromagnetic fields, and that increasing their exposure to them can indeed have demonstrable negative effects.[10] It seems appropriate, at the very least, to extend the remit of the question originally posed by Lyotard to nature and ask:

> What if what is 'proper' to nature were to be inhabited by that which is hostile to nature? What if the living world were to be infiltrated by a force inimical to life?

As we shall see in Chapters Three and Four, the rollout of 5G is premised on a further significant increase in the overall amount of radiofrequency radiation to which the planet will be subjected. 5G will help to establish a global 'electronic ecosystem' that, in addition to servicing the technological desires and aspirations of city-dwellers living in their 'smart homes', will also enable greater monitoring and control of natural ecosystems and living creatures. It involves the insertion of the electronic ecosystem into these natural ecosystems, in order to create a 'smart planet'.

The Western wisdom tradition has long acknowledged two aspects of nature: visible and invisible, or manifest and unmanifest.[11] The physical forms that we perceive in the world around us arise from non-perceptible creative and formative forces, which must be taken into account if we are to grasp things in their wholeness. It is these forces which carry the energies of life, just as surely as electromagnetic radiation opposes them. One of the challenges we face today is to overcome our collective de-sensitization to these subtle life-forces. One step towards doing so is to free ourselves from the dominant utilitarian stance towards nature, which prioritizes data-collection and analysis and ever seeks practical results, but is closed to nature's interiority just as it is closed to the interior of our soul-life. A different kind of consciousness is needed—more receptive, open and empathetic. Regarding this different kind of consciousness, Goethe advised:

> Our full attention must be focused on the task of *listening to nature*, to overhear the secret of her process.[12]

All of creation speaks of a transcendent spiritual intelligence at its source, if only we are able to hear it.[13] The mystical path to union with God has long been understood to lead from the loving contemplation of creatures to the contemplation of this greater spiritual intelligence from which they issue, and on which they, like we, ultimately depend.[14] For human beings to forget or neglect this relationship of nature to the divine is as serious a failing as it is for us to forget our relationship to the spiritual intelligence that dwells within us. To put it in Christian terms, the same Cosmic Logos lives at the very heart of both nature and the human soul.

Contemporary conditions make it very difficult for such perspectives to be taken with the seriousness they deserve. The incursion of the inhuman has allowed the utilitarian mind to break free of the moral and spiritual constraints that once kept it in bounds. But with the burgeoning electronics industry and the drive to forge a 'smart planet', a force hostile to nature insinuates itself into nature's heart. These developments make nature vulnerable to increasing technologization, one example of which is the fabrication of completely new synthetic organisms using computer programs.[15] Another example is the design of remotely controlled robot bees to replace the dwindling number of living bees (discussed in Chapter Four). Such interventions are only the beginning of a vastly ambitious project to redesign the world to satisfy the requirements of a ruthlessly technological consciousness that has lost all connection with its spiritual roots. This consciousness has no sense of the sacredness of life, nor of the spiritual responsibilities of human beings towards nature.

Foremost amongst these responsibilities is the obligation to know things in the truth of their being. Of all creatures on Earth, it is human beings alone who have the possibility of selflessly entering into the inner nature of another creature, without seeking to use or exploit it for our own ends. We alone can place ourselves imaginatively and empathetically into the being of another and, through opening the inner eye of the mind, or heart, we have the possibility of beholding the other in their truth. If we can regularly practise this, then we can help to build up a 'spiritual ecosystem' that can counterbalance the deathly 'electronic ecosystem' currently being established, for our mode of knowing can contribute something positive and life-affirming to the world. It can be a deed of illumination, which gives to nature the gift of our conscious recognition of its sacred ground (discussed in Chapter Five). Human beings and nature belong together. The struggle for a human future is at the same time a struggle for nature's future. Just as we depend on nature for our survival, so too does nature depend on the quality of our knowing and relating, through which we may bring spiritual light to the world.

The essays that follow seek both to highlight the critical challenges that we now face, while also pointing towards ways in which we can positively respond to them. The essays do not have to be read sequentially. They each stand independently of each other. They have, however, been revised, updated and welded together as far as possible into a coherent whole. They are presented in the hope that they will, taken together, encourage the reader to renew his or her commitment to the inner work that is so sorely needed today, in the spirit of Rilke's affirmation:

> The most wonderful aspect of life still seems to me that some coarse and crude intervention and even blatant violation can become the occasion for establishing a new order within us.[16]

Chapter One

TECHNOLOGY AND THE SOUL

Being There

Some years ago, on a trip to Australia, I was told the story of how, sometime in the 1920s, an Aborigine who lived deep in the Outback had his first encounter with modern civilization. He had apparently never been near a city or town and had managed to avoid having any significant contact with Europeans. Then one day he saw a cloud of dust in the distance coming slowly towards him. As it drew nearer he heard a sound that he had never before heard. It was a low growling sound, but not of any living creature. This sound did not express any quality of soul that he recognized. As the growling Thing moved closer, the Aborigine saw that it was not moving like any animal, but came straight towards him with an uncanny deliberateness. The Thing was entirely black, save for parts that flashed and gleamed in the sunlight. The Aborigine stood transfixed, unable to do anything other than watch with increasing trepidation as this noisome, brutish apparition approached him. When at last, full of menace, it loomed up in front of where he stood, belching smoke and fumes, he involuntarily went down on his knees, and in what we must presume was a paroxysm of absolute terror, he died.

This story of the Aborigine whose soul was not strong enough to survive his first encounter with the motorcar poignantly expresses the problem that modern technology presents to us today. The story suggests that, in order to live with motorcars, something in our own souls must die. Something of our own primal humanity must be killed, or at the very least be suppressed. Technology is soulless. But more than that, it has an inimical effect on *our* souls. In order to relate not just to motorcars, but to all the other increasingly sophisticated machines and gadgets that accompany our daily lives, it seems that we must grow distant from that part of our own inner being that instinctively participates in, or feels close to, primordial nature. We become insensitive both to that which is visible and to that which is invisible in nature. The world of machines, almost by definition, requires of us that we close ourselves off from the intrinsic mysteriousness of being alive. And the more sophisticated the machines are, the more our relationship to them induces a certain hardening of our souls: we must lose our 'innocence' in order to be able to live in relation to them.

In a seminal essay, *The Question Concerning Technology*, Martin Heidegger argued that it is contact with our own essence that technology most threatens. It is threatened by what Heidegger calls the rule of *Gestell*, somewhat awkwardly translated as 'enframing'. By *Gestell* we may understand the fixing of things in a framework of meaning that is entirely instrumental to our purposes. Their meaning is to serve us, and they do not have any meaning or value apart from their usefulness to us. Our relationship to them, therefore, does not give us an entry-point to life as such. Rather than evoking in us the experience of wonder at the underlying numinosity of life, our relationship with technology tends to confine us within an artificially constructed human-machine world. And so, to the extent that we depend upon it, we cut ourselves off from something essential to our own nature as human beings. We become peripheral to ourselves, because for Heidegger our essential human nature is precisely an openness to Being, which he defines as 'being-there' (*Da-sein*) or 'being present' to the mystery of existence. In *The Question Concerning Technology*, he writes:

> The threat to man does not come in the first instance from the potentially lethal machines and apparatus of technology. The actual threat has already affected man in his essence. The rule of *Gestell* ['enframing'] threatens man with the possibility that it could be denied to him to enter a more original revealing and hence the call of a more primal truth.[1]

At about the same time as the Aborigine had his confrontation with the motorcar, far away in Switzerland, at Bollingen on the edges of Lake Zürich, the renowned psychologist C. G. Jung built for himself a private retreat (Fig.1.1). It had no electricity or running water and no telephone. For heating, Jung himself chopped wood for the fireplace. Deliberately cutting out all of modern technology, Jung aimed to live as simply as possible at Bollingen, for only in this way could he reconnect with his 'true life'. In his autobiography, *Memories, Dreams and Reflections* he wrote:

> At Bollingen I am in the midst of my true life: I am most deeply myself.[2]

He described it as 'a place of spiritual concentration' where there was 'nothing to disturb the dead':

> If a man of the 16th century were to move into the house, only the kerosene lamp and the matches would be new to him; otherwise he would know his way about without difficulty.[3]

Jung also felt that at Bollingen he could reconnect with the natural world. He felt himself to be

Figure 1.1, Jung's retreat at Bollingen.

spread out over the landscape and inside things... living in every tree, in the splashing of the waves, in the clouds and the animals that come and go, in the procession of the seasons.[4]

At Bollingen, Jung discarded the twentieth century in order to get in touch with his own primitive nature, his 'aboriginal' self. He understood that modern technology drives out the old instinctive participation in the natural world, and tears us away from contact with our soul-life. That is why he found it necessary to return to Bollingen where, through living in utter simplicity, he could reconnect with his own humanity.

It is related that for years the owner of a nearby restaurant, which Jung used to visit, thought Jung was a 'nice old farmer'. They would sit on the cellar stairs, sampling wines and chatting. When informed by some visitors that Jung was a world famous psychologist, the man was amazed.[5] Jung understood that being simple and living close to nature is what really nurtures the inner life. He saw that one of the greatest problems for modern humanity is that our consciousness has 'slipped from its natural foundations.'[6] He wrote:

Natural life is the nourishing soil of the soul.[7]

Today the soul is not nourished as it used to be, and our growing reliance on technology—especially computer technology—is one of the reasons why.

While computer technology clearly brings to humanity many benefits, it is important that we wake up to its shadow side. The extraordinary momentum of the Digital Revolution has meant that it has become embedded in every corner of the day-to-day functioning of contemporary society. But electronic technology's shadow is generally overlooked while every new innovation is welcomed uncritically as bringing improvement to the quality of our lives. There is far too little serious questioning of the effects that the Digital Revolution is having on us—not just physical effects but effects on the human psyche and on our inner attunement to spirit. Evidently, we do not have much choice but to live with computer technology, but we all need to find a way of doing so in which we retain our spiritual freedom and at the same time protect the integrity of the delicate inner world of the psyche. If both of these are threatened, then the fundamental question that faces all of us today is: How can we live with and use this technology in such a way that it does not undermine, but rather helps us to unfold, what is essential to our humanity?

In this chapter I will consider just four shadow aspects of computer technology, which seem to me to be deeply challenging: addiction, psychic fragmentation, abandonment of the real for the virtual and the drift towards becoming cyborg.[8] I believe that they all share one thing in common, which is that they tend to draw us away from 'being-there' in Heidegger's sense. That is to say, they tend to draw us away from a living connectedness to the mystery of existence, and thereby from an essential human experience. For this reason, they present us with the spiritual challenge to strengthen our own latent capacity to, in Heidegger's words, 'enter a more original revealing' and to nurture our own openness to 'the call of a more primal truth'. In the final section I shall address the question of how we can live with computer technology while at the same time holding on to, and indeed deepening, all that belongs to us uniquely as human beings.

Addiction

One of the most obvious hazards of digital technology is addiction. It is probably something that most of us have experienced at first hand. Addiction declares itself in the feeling that we cannot bear to be without the object to which we feel attached. We feel it has become an indispensable part of our life, and that we could not cope, we could not function properly, even that we could not *survive,* without it. Many people have felt this in relation to their digital devices, as we shall see.

In 2006, a survey was conducted on mobile phone use in the United Kingdom.[9] At this time smartphones were a relative novelty. The first BlackBerry smartphone (with the ability to send and receive emails and browse the Internet) only appeared in 2003, and Apple's first iPhone would not be manufactured until 2007. So the survey was mostly of mobile phone use pre-smartphone. The survey produced statistics revealing already a high level of addiction. When deprived of the use of their mobile phone, one quarter of respondents reported feeling 'isolated and out of control', 66% felt 'frustrated and inconvenienced', while a mere 1% felt 'relieved'. This was despite the fact that for thousands upon thousands of years, human beings had managed to live without mobile phones, and never once did anyone have the experience that the lack of a mobile phone caused them to feel isolated, out of control, frustrated or inconvenienced (or, for that matter, relieved).

In 2016, ten years later, another survey was conducted—this time including smartphone use.[10] It found that, on average, adults were spending 25 hours a week online, in other words just over a day a week. It also found that the majority (59%) of Internet users regarded themselves as 'hooked'. Excessive checking of one's connected device is a typical symptom; finding it hard to disconnect is another; feeling nervous or anxious when offline is another common symptom.[11] Clearly, our reliance on digital technology has negative effects on our wellbeing and sense of inner balance.

In the 2016 survey, half of smartphone users admitted that they slept with their phone beside their bed, and just under half said that the last thing they did before they went to sleep and the first thing they did when they woke was to check their phone. The survey also revealed that for many, if they woke in the dead of night, the first thing they did was to check their phone (Fig. 1.2).[12] In the Western monastic tradition these times just before sleeping and waking, as well as in the very middle of the night, are regarded as the most spiritually potent times, each dedicated to prayer and the 'inner turn' towards the centre. Surveys such as this show the degree to which the technology has come to occupy areas of the soul-life that previously were reserved for spiritual practice.

One of the most sensitive commentators on the Digital Revolution, the social psychologist Sherry Turkle, pointed out that our digital devices have become like extensions of our minds, 'poised between the world of the animate and inanimate... experienced as both part of the self and of the external world'.[13] We want them close to us because we feel they hold something of our identity: we feel they are our 'second self'—hence the

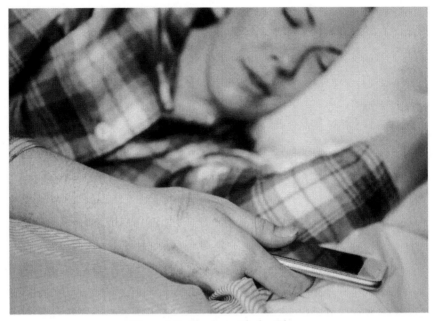

Figure.1.2, Sleeping with the iPhone.

panic when we lose them or when they crash. If we wake in the night, we check the phone in order to reconnect ourselves with the ground of our life. But is it the true ground? And is this digital second self the self we are really seeking to connect with? Some people, at least, are coming to understand our dependency on our digital devices is ultimately an illusion, and that their grip on us dissolves when we spend time away from their influence. The 2016 survey reported that there appeared to be a growing awareness of the value of deliberately taking a break from spending time online, with one third of those who did so saying that they felt more productive, and around a quarter saying they found it liberating.[14]

In another essay, Heidegger argued that technology itself, in so far as we come to rely on it, induces in us what he referred to as 'an increasingly hardened forgetfulness of Being'.[15] The reason is that the more technology infiltrates our lives, the more we orientate ourselves *towards it* rather than towards the remembrance of Being. We become dependent on something outside us, investing it with a power that should rightly be claimed as our own. A certain weakness insinuates itself into the soul and becomes lodged there, having the effect that our sense of equanimity is no longer securely anchored, but is upset by the relatively trivial circumstance of being deprived of these ultimately inessential adjuncts to our lives. Technology enthrals us, but the more enthralled we become, the more distance we put between ourselves and that with which Jung sought to connect at Bollingen in his electricity- and telephone-free tower.

It is important to remember that mobile connectivity has not been with us for very long. Mobile phones are phenomena of the 1990s, and smartphones with Internet capabilities took off in the following decade. And yet they have swiftly become all-pervasive, and regarded by many people as indispensable to daily life. But the time will come when smartphones too will be a thing of the past, superseded by wearable devices. While there is no doubting the usefulness of digital technology, to the extent that we become reliant on it we become reliant on something transient and essentially extraneous to ourselves. And if we become over reliant on it, so that our digital devices become our constant referent, then we may lose our own inner moorings. The danger is that we are pulled away from our own centre. We become alienated from nature, unable to endure solitude, unable to endure inactivity. We lose the secret of our own peace.

Psychic Fragmentation

One of the consequences of the Digital Revolution is that we have all become *interruptible*, especially if we are inclined never to turn our device (or devices) off. The age of mobile communication has been wittily christened by *New York Times* columnist Thomas Friedman 'The Age of Interruption', because if someone else is not interrupting us we are—as likely as not—interrupting them.[16] No matter where we are, no matter what we are doing or who we are with, our space is no longer inviolable. Friedman reminds his readers that not so long ago, before mobile phones, when you went 'out', then you were unobtainable. If someone wanted to contact you, they would have to wait until your return. Even when you were 'in', there were areas in the house and times of day when you were effectively 'out'—not reachable. It is still possible to live in this way, even if only a minority choose to do so. Turning the phone off is still an option. The revolution in communications technologies has, however, meant that being constantly reachable—and also being able to reach others—has become the new social norm.

This has resulted in our lives becoming more and more fragmented. The psychic space that we create when we are talking with a friend, walking in a wood, or reading a book, is a space that is not protected as it used to be. It can suddenly be torn into by literally anyone who wants to contact us. What suffers here is introversion. Modern communications technology works against the creation of secure places where the mood of introversion can be nurtured. While we have the option to turn our devices off, the expectations that they have created in a society that has all too eagerly embraced what they have to offer conspire to make us keep them on. We therefore find ourselves drawn towards an increasingly extroverted lifestyle, in which the possibilities of deepening our communion with nature, with our friends, with ourselves, and with the inner worlds of psyche and spirit, are all subtly curtailed.

In this respect, digital technologies have undoubtedly affected the quality of consciousness that we bring to the tasks and the varied encounters of our daily life. Most spiritual traditions emphasize the importance of cultivating the ability to give single-minded attention to whatever it is we are doing, as one of the foundations of the spiritual life. The Buddha called it Right Mindfulness (or Right Attentiveness), and described the true aspirant as one who 'in walking, in standing, in sitting; in falling asleep, in waking; in speaking or in keeping silence. In all of these he applies full attention.'[17] Mobile digital technologies encourage us to divide our attention, and to do more than one thing at a time. Inevitably, we then act with less than full attention. The term 'multitasking' describes the state of soul that many of us feel obliged to adopt. This term was invented specifically to describe the parallel functioning of computer operations, and was first used in a 1960s IBM instruction manual.[18] Multitasking is something humans are now all expected to be able to do—it has become normal, even an ability to be proud of, but it comes at the cost of the quality of our attentiveness. Thomas Friedman, in the article to which I have just referred, declared that the type of consciousness that the new technologies promote is one of 'continuous partial attention.' They tend to steer us away from being centred and focused, and increase within us a desire, or even need, for distraction. In this way they undermine, rather than help, to secure the foundations of the spiritual life.

It is not that the technology in itself is to blame for our increased distractedness. We are all susceptible to distraction; we all have the tendency to be less than fully focused and to try to do more than one thing at a time. It is not easy to anchor oneself in oneself, giving each activity or task one's sustained and undivided attention. A certain amount of effort is therefore demanded of us in order to practise Right Mindfulness. My point is simply that information/communication/entertainment technologies do not help us to make this effort. They tend rather to play to our weaknesses than to our strengths. In the end, it is of course we who bear responsibility for whether we surrender to our weaknesses or find the strength to overcome them.

And in so far as we do not allow ourselves to be scattered by the technology but make it an instrument of our own deeper human goals, the technology itself could be said to achieve a kind of redemption.[19]

Continuous partial attention is, however, at one end of a spectrum, the other end of which is potentially far more damaging to the psyche. The Internet has given us the possibility of recreating ourselves as a virtual persona, or as multiple personae with different identities, in online chat rooms, social networks, computer games and virtual communities. It has enabled us to reinvent ourselves as anyone we choose to become in the online environment. In 1993, at around the time when the Internet began to be used more widely, a cartoon appeared in the *New Yorker* showing two dogs, one with its paw on the keyboard of a computer. This dog gleefully explains to the dog sitting beside him the benefits of the Internet: 'On the Internet, nobody knows you're a dog.' (Fig. 1.3). The Internet gives us the possibility of cloaking ourselves in the figures of our fantasy. It could be argued that this enables people to explore their sub-personalities in a potentially healthy way. But then, of course, if everyone is exploring his or her sub-personalities online, who in the end is communicating with whom? *Who* is really there? Do these online experiences of oneself lead towards greater psychic integration or greater psychic fragmentation?

The booming industry of video games and virtual worlds, from World of Warcraft and Star Wars to Second Life, Entropia and Habbo, for which one must create an avatar (or online representative of oneself) in order to interact with the virtual domain, makes these questions all the more pressing. Avatars, like the characters a novelist invents, have a way of quickly assuming a reality independent of their creator. They may come to haunt us in our 'offline' hours in powerful and unsettling ways. Because the avatar is a projection of oneself—or an aspect of oneself—one may come to feel intimately connected with it, potentially investing in it one's unexpressed drives, aspirations and fantasies. We enter a realm of mirrors, in which powerful psychological complexes may be prematurely released from the protective veils of the unconscious, and assume an apparently objective existence before a person is inwardly strong enough to deal with them.[20]

One aspect of this is that a person may come to identify more and more with their avatar, feeling that they can be more truly themselves through their online persona than in real life. It is not uncommon for people to say and do things through their avatar that they would only dream of saying or doing in the real world. While this may have some therapeutic value, the ultimate challenge remains to be able to live fully in the real world. The attraction of

Figure.1.3, On the Internet, nobody knows you're a dog.

the virtual world has something of the quality of our dream-life. As more and more people acquire avatars, there is a danger of some losing the boundaries of their self-identity and in the process losing their relationship to reality. Because the avatar is by definition not one's physical body, yet at the same time constitutes one's online identity, it can lure us into *really* inhabiting (that is, with psychological commitment) a world that is essentially *not real*—a world that is an artificial, machine construct, that could be snuffed out the very second the electricity supply fails.

Much work has been invested in enabling people to create lifelike avatars of themselves, so that experiences in virtual worlds (for example 'avatar video conferencing') can become more realistic.[21] One research goal of tech companies is to be able to bind the avatar ever more closely to the person whose avatar it is, so that it becomes a second electronic 'incarnation' of the person. For example, a headset can scan activity in the brain's motor cortex (which controls voluntary movement of limbs) so that when a person focuses on moving their feet, their *avatar's* feet will move, when they focus on moving their hands, their *avatar's* hands will move.[22] Facebook's 'Reality Labs' are currently working on a project called 'Codec Avatars', which is devising methods of making much more lifelike virtual representations of a person, using 3D capture technology and AI systems. The aim is to render 'realistic virtual humans'—that is, to recreate a person in an electronic body down to the recognizable wrinkle of the face or smallest gesture, so that virtual interactions will eventually become indistinguishable from real ones. All you would need to do is put on a headset and you could meet people thousands of miles away, appearing to them, moving and sounding just like you do in real life.[23] Only it will not be you, it will be your avatar, your electronic doppelgänger. But people may nevertheless come to feel that this electronic body is as much theirs as is their physical body. One objective of current research is that we shall learn to inhabit the electronic body of our avatar. We shall, in effect, become adjusted to having two bodies: a physical body for the real world and an electronic body for the virtual world. A kind of technology-induced schizophrenia will ensue. Which body is our real body? Which world is the real world?

Abandoning the Real for the Virtual

We have seen that in 2016, on average, adults were spending roughly 25 hours a week online, in other words just over a day a week, or 54 days a year. According to a survey conducted ten years previously, they were spending just under 42 days a year.[24] The trend is likely to continue to be towards more and more time spent online, especially given the current direction of research that we have been considering. As we have seen, the goal of the tech companies is to make virtual interactions indistinguishable from real ones. Our future is that we shall all become 'digital citizens'. And as the amount of time spent online increases, the amount of time spent relating to our physical environment diminishes. According to the National Trust, in 2016 British children spent half the time their parents did playing outside. What were they doing instead? They were watching films or playing computer games.[25] How, then, can we expect them to grow up caring about their fellow creatures in the wild, caring about frogs and birds, squirrels and foxes, mountains, rivers, wild flowers and forests? The consequence of spending more and more time online is that people's knowledge of, sensitivity towards, and ability to relate to, nature also diminishes. The more we become 'digital citizens', the less we feel ourselves to be citizens of the natural world.

E. M. Forster describes the dystopian future we are heading for very evocatively in his novella *The Machine Stops*, first published in 1909. His story is of people living in a society that no longer exists on the surface of the earth but has established itself underground. Completely disconnected from nature, human beings dwell within the belly of a massive computer network, an underground machine. They live with minimal physical contact in their own isolated individual cells, communicating with each other through the medium of their electrical apparatus of 'speaking tubes' and a video connection device. The latter is the primary source of entertainment and information as well as visual communication with other people. At the end of the story the machine breaks down, and the civilization that has embraced the illusion that it can exist apart from nature and apart from genuine human contact implodes.

Forster's prophetic story has increasing relevance to us. The number of virtual communities has been steadily rising over the years. By 2019, there were over 300 virtual communities, accessible only through a computer connection.[26] Their creation is a step towards the world that he describes in *The Machine Stops*. One of the turning points in our relationship to virtuality was when it became possible to make real money by buying and selling virtual goods and services. Virtual communities evolved real economies where real profits could be made. Once people could actually make a living in the virtual world, buying and selling virtual land, virtual houses, virtual clothes and so on, then the virtual exercised a gravitational pull far greater than it had done previously. Although it may be literally true that virtual goods are nothing more than computer codes, they have value in the imagination and in the desires of those who buy and sell them. Consider the following examples of landmark transactions: in October 2005 someone bought a virtual asteroid in the Swedish virtual world, *Entropia*, for $100,000 to develop it as a virtual space resort. In November 2010, an *Entropia* virtual club called 'Club Neverdie' was sold for $635,000. In 2014, the virtual world *Planet Arkadia* started selling Arkadia Underground Deeds valued at $5 each, making the Arkadia Underground worth $1 million.[27] The value of virtual planets, virtual space stations and virtual resorts is premised on the fact that a fairly large number of human beings identify so strongly with the world of their avatars that the idea of spending time on a

virtual asteroid, in a virtual club or space resort actually carries significant meaning for them. One of the most telling examples of the degree
of psychological commitment that virtual worlds can command is a pur-
chase from 2007, when the virtual world *There* teamed up with Levi's
to make virtual versions of Levi clothing for their avatar population. A
virtual Levi jacket was, astonishingly, sold for $83—more than the cost of
the equivalent real jacket.[28] To clothe one's avatar at such expense implies
an almost touching vanity on behalf of one's online persona.

Why would anyone want to do that? Why is it that computer games
and virtual communities hold such a powerful attraction for people? The
reason, I suspect, is that these worlds present to us an apparently objective
realm of images that reminds us of the inner psychic world. For Jung, as for
Henry Corbin and those mystical traditions that honour both the image
and the cognitive faculty of the imagination, the realm of images can serve
as the mediator between the human soul and deeper archetypal realities. As
such, it promises to put us in touch with a numinous archetypal or spiritual
content. The danger of machine-generated virtual worlds is that the human
being is seduced by a counterfeit realm of images—a counterfeit *mundus
imaginalis*—that does not open to any numinous content.[29] Instead, people
become lost in materialistic fantasies of buying and selling dream houses
on virtual asteroids or dressing their virtual alter ego in clothing that they
probably would not themselves ever dare to actually wear. No doubt many
also give in to the temptation to virtually do all sorts of illicit things that
they would not do in real life.

One pointer towards this degradation of the inner life of the soul is the
quality of the image with which one is interacting in virtual worlds. In
those mystical traditions that honour the image, great care and devotion
goes into the creation of sacred images. This is because an image worthy
of contemplation needs to be created from a contemplative and prayerful
state of soul. Only then will it have the spiritual capacity to lead the one
who contemplates it towards a deeper truth. The machine-generated image,
which characteristically has a cartoon-like quality, is the opposite of sacred
art. Even with the increasing sophistication and realism of computer-
generated images, the inherent quality of digital media is that—precisely by
being electronic—they cannot rise to the level of sacred art, for the fundamental gesture of the electronic is to close us off from objective spiritual
reality. Rather, to live with such images day after day only leads to a coars-
ening of that most precious of human faculties—the imagination, with its
inherent visionary potential.

Becoming Cyborg

Psychotherapists report that it is increasingly common for characters and scenes from computer games and virtual worlds to populate their clients' dreams. If the unconscious is more and more to be permeated by imagery of machine-derivation, then this constitutes a grave intrusion into the inner lives of human beings. It seems that there is now a very real prospect that machine-generated virtual worlds will become not simply worlds that we inhabit but worlds that *inhabit us*, by insinuating themselves into both our conscious and unconscious lives, affecting our values, our judgements and our perceptions.

One of the promises of 5G is that it will enable computer-generated content to be more readily accommodated within our daily experience through Augmented Reality (AR) technologies. The so-called 'augmentation' of experience with digital overlays has become relatively common now, allowing people to look through their smartphone at computer graphics and information superimposed on their actual experience of the world. *Google Skymap*, for example, is one of several AR applications that overlays information about the stars as the viewer points the camera of their smartphone or tablet towards a particular area of the sky. The game *Pokémon Go* is another example of AR in action. It became hugely popular because it gave players the ability to see virtual Pokémon creatures in real physical locations through their smartphones (Fig.1.4). But this is just the beginning. Because 5G promises to enable far greater amounts of data to be processed at much higher speeds, the world will become increasingly permeated with virtual content to be retrieved with Augmented Reality applications. This will provide a strong impetus for the replacement of portable computers like the smartphone, tablet and laptop with wearable devices like smartglasses and headsets (see Chapter Three).

The wearable computer will not, however, be the endpoint. It should be seen as a step on the way to a biologically integrated computer. The more we identify ourselves as 'digital citizens' living in a dual world in which virtual and real intermingle, the more we shall find ourselves channelled towards biological integration of computer technology. Preparations for this have long been underway. The so-called 'bionic contact lens', for example, was first developed at the University of Washington in 2008.[30] It has an imprinted electronic circuit only a few nanometres thick, and is combined with microscopic light-emitting diodes (Fig. 1.5). Because these components are so small, they do not obstruct a person's view, but they do allow virtual displays to be projected in front of the eye, which only the wearer of

Figure 1.4, Pokémon Go: virtual reality enters physical space.

the lens would perceive. This enables the wearer of the lens to live in their private virtual world, much as headphones allow the wearer to listen to private audio content. By 2016, the University of Washington research team had developed wireless connectivity between the lens and smartphones and smartwatches, thereby providing Internet access.[31]

As time goes on, such interfaces will become increasingly refined. They will radically transform our daily experience, for not only will our environment be a hybrid of virtual and real, but our inner life of thoughts, feelings, desires and intentions will inevitably be transformed by the hybrid perceptions that will constitute the reality in which we shall live. Earlier, I referred to the development of a headset that scans areas of the brain's motor cortex, thereby giving a person control over the movement of their avatar in a virtual world through focusing attention on different parts of their own physical body. For many years now, work has been progressing towards the development of the so-called 'brain-chip', or neural interface, that connects the human brain to a computer. Implanted in the motor cortex, the chip's electronic sensors detect brain-cell activity, which is translated into digital output signals that can then, for example, move a cursor, or replicate keystrokes on a computer screen. Thus, by the power of thought alone, a person becomes able to operate a computer, smartglasses or a robot.[32]

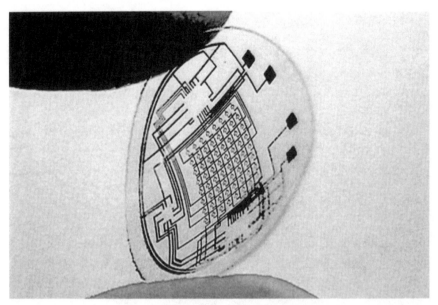

Figure 1.5, The University of Washington's bionic contact lens with imprinted electronic circuit and light-emitting diodes.

One of the driving forces behind research into neural interface technology has been the desire to help the severely disabled, but much of the funding for it in the United States has come from the main research organization of the United States Department of Defence, DARPA (Defence Advanced Research Projects Agency).[33] Neural interface technology has obvious military applications that extend into spheres far removed from their apparently benign medical alias of assisting paraplegics. From a military point of view the ability to control, by the power of thought alone, machines that kill is clearly a prize worth investing millions of dollars to attain.

What we are considering here is the augmentation of the powers of the human mind, but without any parallel ethical development of the human being. From a traditional religious standpoint, or equally from a modern esoteric standpoint, any increase in human mental capacities should only be sought in conjunction with the transformation of one's shadow. It demands the stringent discipline of self-honesty, along with the thorough integration of, and commitment to, the highest moral standards, not least of which is that we do no harm to others. Brain-machine interface technology, which (as we shall see in the next chapter) will incorporate neural Internet connections, contains the inherent risk of artificially endowing human beings with abilities akin to clairvoyance, telepathic communication and enhanced powers of memory, without any accompanying moral develop-ment.[34] This leads to the danger not only that people will more easily cause harm to others, but that they will also more easily cause harm to them-selves. When this technology becomes generally available, it will carry an irresistible allure to those who seek to augment their mental capacities, but who lack moral maturity, and may also lack awareness of the reality of the psychic and spiritual dimensions. Such people could completely lose their grounding in truly human goals and values.

There is little doubt that as time goes on we shall witness an increas-ing pressure on human beings to become ever more closely merged with machines. Transhumanists are convinced not only that an increasing incor-poration of computer-based technologies into our bodies and minds will happen, but that this is also something which we should positively wel-come.[35] This attitude is becoming increasingly widespread and is no longer regarded as controversial. For example, in 2019 an influential Royal Society report advocated that a national 'neural interface ecosystem' be set up in the UK to accelerate development of these technologies, and envisaged increasing collaboration between medical and gaming communities to fur-ther the development of neural interface applications.[36]

It is quite possible that those who embrace the merger with machines may be endowed with an apparent enhancement of their cognitive pow-ers. But this enhancement will be a technological, not a moral or spiritual achievement, and as such it is more likely to confine them within what Heidegger called 'the rule of *Gestell*' than open them up to genuine aware-ness of the spiritual realm. Technological enhancement is an invitation to the inhuman to take up residence within the soul. Those who invite the inhuman to dwell within them take the risk, to use Heidegger's words, of being denied the possibility 'to enter a more original revealing' and unable to respond to 'the call of a more primal truth.' They risk severing them-selves from the very essence of what it means to be human.

The Saving Power

At the beginning of this chapter, we saw that for Heidegger the threat to humanity does not come in the first instance from 'the potentially lethal apparatus of technology'. It comes from the corruption of the human essence, in which people sacrifice their intrinsic openness to the mystery of existence for the sake of a merely instrumental relationship to the world. We could equally say that in this scenario the values of the spiritual con-templative, which are to give understanding, empathy and love to the other, are made secondary to the technological attitude that seeks to gain greater power, mastery and control of the world. When we allow the technological attitude to dominate, then we expose the most precious thing in ourselves to corruption.

Towards the end of his essay, Heidegger quotes the poet Hölderlin, who wrote:

> But where danger is,
> grows the saving power also.[37]

Heidegger asks: how do we foster the growth of this saving power? His answer is that it may be fostered through the arts, because the arts can awaken in us that openness to the mystery of existence that is essential to our being human. It is with this potent thought that Heidegger's essay concludes, leaving us with an important indicator as to the direction that we need to go in if we are to preserve essential human values while at the same time living with, and benefiting from, computer technology. The solution to the problem that this technology presents can only be one that brings us back to ourselves, to nurturing within ourselves what belongs to us inherently as human beings.

With regard to the addictive nature of digital technology, Heidegger is surely right. Practically, speaking, we can foster the saving power by building into our daily lives artistic experiences that are not machine-mediated, and that put us in touch with our own vitality: through music—that is through playing actual musical instruments, and singing—through painting, drawing and sculpting, through the art of conversation, through writing and reading poetry, and a host of other activities, in which we make contact with the sources of creativity within us. Thereby we can to some extent counteract the tendency to become addicted to our machines, and to machine-mediated communication and entertainment.

The tendency to psychic fragmentation, however, presents us with a different level of challenge that needs to be met with a different level of response. The practice of giving full attention to whatever it is we are doing (i.e. the cultivation of mindfulness) is an inner discipline that is vital if we are to hold our own in the face of the multiple demands on our attention that stream towards us. But the problem of psychic fragmentation also includes our relationship to potentially multiple virtual personae and sub-personae. These inevitably challenge us to consider our deeper identity, or what might be called our authentic self. One response to this challenge is to sharpen our moral consciousness, so that this accompanies us into virtual worlds just as it does in the real world, for no matter who or what we (in whatever guise) are interacting with, it is always *we* who are doing the interacting, and therefore we need to guard our moral integrity. To sustain an intrinsic moral sense in whatever situation we find ourselves—whether virtual or real—is a way of fostering the saving power, for it means centring ourselves in the unifying core of goodness, which is the birthright of every human being.

The third hazard of technology—that it tempts us away from the real into a virtual world, so that we not only disengage from nature but also become alienated from the reality of our own inner life—presents us with a further challenge that we can meet only through further intensification of our own inner activity. First of all, we can cultivate a greater awareness of and sensitivity to nature. Given the unfolding ecological crisis, this surely is an obligation that we all have. We can fulfil this obligation in simple ways, for instance by deliberately spending more time outside, going for walks, making a point of observing and getting to know the plants and animals, the winds and different kinds of cloud, the stars and planets, that are our constant companions. Then we may come to stand within the mystery of existence, and this will have its effect, not just on us but on nature too. And if we have gardens or land, then there is much we can practically do to help nature. Given the tendency for our relationship to nature to be pushed to the margins of our lives through excessive engagement with computer-mediated experiences, it is all the more important that we make the effort to bring our focus back to real reality.

Secondly, alongside this nurturing of a more conscious relationship to nature, we need for the sake of our souls to attend to our own inner world of images—both to the spontaneous imagery of our dreams and also to the treasury of religious and archetypal images and symbols, neither of which are machine-mediated and both of which have the capacity to connect us with the true as opposed to the counterfeit imaginal world. By actively living what Jung called 'the symbolic life' we can nurture in ourselves the ability to discriminate between what genuinely connects us with a deeper level of reality and what takes us into the merely fantastical.[38]

The fourth hazard of technology—'becoming cyborg'—presents an even more fundamental challenge. Because the direction of digital technology is towards increasing intimacy between ourselves and our digital devices, we need humanly to constantly check our boundaries with the gadgets and devices that we use, clearly establishing where we 'are' in relation to them. One question we can repeatedly ask ourselves is: Is what I am doing coming fully from myself, or am I acting under the influence of thoughts, desires and motivations stimulated in me by the machine? For the sake of maintaining our own freedom, we need to keep establishing and re-establishing our experience of what is truly 'I', in the higher sense of the word, and what is 'not-I'. If, as seems inevitable, in the future the pressure intensifies to integrate more closely with machines, this is an essential criterion to bring to every decision concerning our relationship to new technologies.

The medieval theologian, Thomas Aquinas, made a distinction that is helpful in this context. He distinguished between our semi-conscious acts, like scratching ourselves or yawning, and those acts that we perform in full consciousness, deliberately and with clear intention. The former he called *actus hominis* or 'acts of man' (in the generic sense), while the latter he termed *actus humani* or 'human acts' in which we act with our full humanity.[39] The distinction is pertinent because in our relations with computer-based technologies today, we are very easily lulled into acting beneath our full human potential, carried away from free and purposeful use of the machine by the plethora of distractions it has to offer us. That we fall asleep to our own deeper motives and intentions is one of the greatest dangers of this technology. In our dealings with it, therefore, we need to conduct ourselves in such a way that our freedom of will, our sense of moral alertness, and our wakefulness to truly human values, remain fully intact, and do not suffer compromise. Acting on this basis, so that our actions are raised to the level of *actus humani*, we may then win a degree of redemption not only for ourselves but also for the technology.

Chapter Two

THE QUEST FOR THE PEARL

Kali Yuga

In ancient Hindu tradition, history is said to unfold in four ages or *yugas*. The first is a long 'golden age' (*Krita Yuga*) when people live in harmony with the gods and the cosmos, scarcely aware of the physical dimension. Through succeeding ages (the *Treta Yuga*, the *Devapara Yuga* and finally the *Kali Yuga*) human beings become increasingly distanced from the spiritual realms, and become more and more attached to the material world. *Kali Yuga* brings this to a culmination: it is the age when awareness of spirit is totally eclipsed, as human consciousness becomes ever more circumscribed by material conditions. Looking upon the material world as the only reality, we forget our divine origins.[1]

At the same time, *Kali Yuga* is the age of ego-consciousness when, having lost awareness of the gods, people gain awareness of their own separate individuality. Having succumbed to the influence of the principle of separation—separation not just from the divine world but also from the spirit within nature—human beings feel they stand alone in the world, and live all too often only for themselves. This accentuated experience of separateness brings in its wake war, social chaos, famine, and ecological disasters on a massive scale.

A further characteristic of *Kali Yuga* is that it is the shortest of the four ages. So time is speeded up: everything happens faster, and people live less long. Not only time but space too is compressed. The world becomes more and more dense, more and more solidified, for it is no longer permeated by spiritual light.[2] And because it is no longer spiritually translucent, people lose their sense of wonder. Even children, to whom wonder comes so naturally, are infected by an increasing cynicism and jadedness in their attitude to life.

This view of history as involving a slow descent from the divine world and a gradual encrustation of the human spirit in matter is not just of Hindu origin. One finds an almost identical teaching in the eighth century BC Greek poet Hesiod, who talks of a comparable decline through a golden age, silver age, bronze age, age of heroes to a final iron age.[3] A similar perspective existed in many ancient cultures. Both the ancient Mesopotamians and the ancient Egyptians had a broadly equivalent view, and we also find something like it in the Persian *Zendavesta*.[4]

So how did those ancient cultures relate to the historical process? At the beginning of *Kali Yuga*, the major preoccupation of ancient societies was to try to hold back the degenerative, downward flow of history. In Egypt, for example, there was a constant attempt to bring the present time into relationship with the 'First Time', when humans lived in the lap of the gods. Each coronation of a new king was seen as an opportunity to restore the whole country to harmony with the cosmos again—to restore it to *Maat*, the cosmic order. Similarly, in the temples, the purpose of the daily temple rituals was to maintain the presence of the gods on earth: there was a sustained effort to stem the tide of history that was running away from contact with the divine world.[5]

This perspective on history differs radically from the view of history prevalent today. But if the defining characteristic of *Kali Yuga* is forgetfulness of the our divine origins, then one should not be surprised if it is difficult for those living in *Kali Yuga's* shadow to understand the ancient perspective. Since it sees us as having descended from a more elevated spiritual state, if such a state no longer has meaning for us, then how could it form part of our understanding of the historical process? The orthodox scientific view today is rather that we have *ascended* from a prior apelike condition, and struggled up through barbarity to our present condition of civilization. It is surely a sign that we are living in the shadow of *Kali Yuga* when people don't talk about the gods, but about their standard of living, about the health service, and about the latest communications technologies. Overshadowed by *Kali Yuga*, we are fixated on the idea of progress, conceived almost entirely in material terms. The ancient cultures are seen as ignorant and superstitious, and the last thing anyone wants to do is to *go back*—and certainly not to some hypothetical palaeolithic golden age.

But the fact that we no longer look back with longing, and seek to return to a previous condition, could be seen as a sign that we are beginning to emerge from *Kali Yuga*. It no longer would make any sense for us to attempt, as the ancient Egyptians did, to hold back the flow of history. We feel we have to work now towards the future. At the same time, if some of us feel inclined to acknowledge and to draw on the rich treasury of wisdom from the past in order to work towards our future, then that could also be taken as a sign that we are beginning to emerge from the grip of the current dark age. The specific dates of *Kali Yuga* are not generally agreed upon. According to modern esotericism, it began shortly before 3000 BC, and was set to last last about five thousand years.[6] But the emergence from *Kali Yuga* is not fore-ordained: it is up to us. We have to make it happen, and if we fail to do so, there will be no new dawn.

The Hymn of the Pearl

If we accept the validity of the general perspective on human history as involving a decline or descent from a previous state of spiritual bliss and harmony with the divine, then there is a very specific question that arises. The question is: what has been the point of this whole process? And if we are now struggling to emerge from *Kali Yuga,* then where exactly do we go from here? By way of answering this question, we can turn to *The Hymn of the Pearl.* It is a story that originated in ancient Persia, and subsequently became absorbed in the later Gnostic tradition. It survives in both a Syriac and a Greek version.[7]

The story tells of a young prince who spends his childhood blissfully happy in the home of his parents, surrounded by an atmosphere of light and love. He wears a beautiful garment made of woven light. But when he grows up, his parents send him away on a mission. He has to 'go down' into a foreign country and bring back a pearl, which is guarded by a very large and ugly serpent monster that lives in the midst of a bustling city. It is a long and arduous journey, and in order to embark on it the prince has to take off his garment of light. The way is described as 'dangerous and harsh' and one must suppose that the prince is tempted many times to turn back, abandon the journey and return to his parents without the pearl.

Nevertheless, he persists and at last arrives in the foreign city where the serpent resides, and where everyone seems to have fallen under its power. In order not to look like a foreigner and arouse people's suspicions, the prince dresses himself in clothes like theirs, woven of ordinary cloth. He goes to stay at an inn, and in case anyone should suspect him of coming to steal the precious pearl, he mingles with the people, and eats and drinks with them there at the inn. And then he falls into a state of profound slumber. He forgets that he is a prince, he forgets that he has a mission. He too falls under the spell of the serpent.

Meanwhile, his parents in the world of light become concerned, and they send an eagle with a message to him to wake up and remember he is a prince, remember that he used to wear a robe woven of light, remember that he has a task to fulfil. When the eagle finds him, asleep at the inn, it rouses him, and the prince does remember who he is and what he is there for. He gets up, summons his courage, and goes to confront the serpent that is coiled around the pearl. Simply by reciting the names of his heavenly mother and father, he is able to overpower the serpent. Then he takes the pearl. He casts off the clothes he has put on, and the eagle now guides him back to his homeland. There he dresses himself again in his garment of woven light, which has become even brighter and more radiant, because of his victorious travails, and he is received jubilantly by the king and queen to whom he gives the pearl.

In this story we see how, at the beginning, the prince lives in a state of blissful but unconscious union with the Mother/Father God. He is then sent down into the foreign land in order that he find *through his own efforts* the spiritual pearl that has become imprisoned within the material world, and return with it to his divine parents. His task can be understood as being to liberate something of the divine nature that has immeasurable value, but lies spellbound within the world.

But we also see that there are dangers involved in this whole enterprise. Two dangers in particular. First of all, there is the danger that the prince, on the outward journey, would find it too hard. Instead of going on down into the foreign land, there is the danger that he might *turn back too soon*. This could be seen as the temptation of the cultures at the beginning of *Kali Yuga* like ancient Egypt, that sought to slow down or even reverse the journey of descent into materiality. Ancient spirituality was based on a yearning to return to the stars, to reunite with heaven, but this involved the temptation to return before a real separation had occurred, with the consequence that the pearl would not be won.[8] The second danger is that the prince, once having entered the foreign country and having experienced separation from the divine world of his origins, should completely forget his true identity and higher purpose. We could surmise that the divine mother and father are taking an enormous risk, a cosmic gamble, in sending the prince out on this mission because the divine parents might completely lose their child to the realm of the serpent. And then the precious pearl would remain within the serpent's coils.

In metaphysical or cosmological terms, then, we could say that the relationship between humanity and the divine world is acted out between a polarity of two quite different and potentially—but not necessarily—contrary desires or longings. On the one hand, there is *the longing to return* to our divine origins. While essentially healthy, this can manifest in an unwholesome, world-rejecting type of spirituality. The danger is that we return too soon or in the wrong way. On the other hand, there is the *pull towards separation* from the spiritual world, so as to stand in complete independence from any relationship to the spiritual. Again, while it is in itself a basically healthy impulse, it carries with it the danger that, in turning away, we separate so completely that we lose all possibility of finding the path back. What is needed is the kind of separation that leads to a free and fully conscious return. Only then can the pearl be truly won.

The Dream of Disincarnation

I have characterized the first tendency, the longing to return, as being especially strong at the beginning of the cycle, in the phase of the journey of the human spirit away from the divine world, and especially as it enters the age of *Kali Yuga*. It manifests as a reluctance to engage with the material world, and as a longing for our cosmic home in the stars. But in modern times, the impulse is still there, and one can see it erupt in a number of different ways today.

For example, there is a current of thought within evangelical Christianity, particularly influential in the United States, that looks forward to the final Apocalypse when true believers will be transported instantly to heaven, in a state of rapture. The rest of us will be left to experience a miserable fate, as the world inexorably descends into chaos. While it is conceived in different ways by different sects, 'the rapture' expresses the dangerous fantasy of a privileged few abandoning the Earth, a fantasy that involves the denial that the Earth is the essential matrix within which human destiny has to be fulfilled. This fantasy, in its most extreme form, lay behind several mass suicides of members of small cults during the 1990s—cults like Solar Temple in Switzerland and Heaven's Gate in the USA, in which members believed that they were the 'chosen few', and that by committing suicide they would each release their spirit to travel to the stars, a journey crudely conceived as aided by extra-terrestrials.[9]

But there is also a technological equivalent of the rapture. It can be seen in the image of the astronaut, who has escaped gravity and floats freely above the Earth. Figure 2.1 shows the astronaut Bruce McCandless during the 1984 Space Shuttle Challenger mission, undergoing an experience previously reserved for shamans and mystics. Now this experience is vouchsafed to the new technological shaman, who enacts the collective dream of disincarnation and abandonment of the Earth. The astronaut has, as Robert Romanyshyn pointed out, become an unconscious fantasy image, the model of new Technological Humanity.[10] Since the 1970s, when the first serious designs of orbiting space stations were made, the prospect of opening up the experience of space flight to more people, though still a select few, has slowly gained traction. In 1999, Kawasaki designed a space hotel, referred to as 'Hotel Galactica', that would be up and running by the year 2020. Despite the 20 year wait, six thousand hopeful Germans made reservations costing £300 each.[11] While this particular project seems to have vanished without trace, the idea of 'space tourism' has steadily grown in popularity, and as if in fulfilment of the dream of Hotel Galactica, NASA announced in June 2019 that the International Space Station would be open to tourists from 2020. The price tag would only be $35,000 per night! However, this excludes the not inconsiderable additional cost of getting there and back, currently estimated to be in the region of $60 million (Fig. 2.2).[12] Private companies are not far behind. Orion Span aims to offer accommodation in its planned orbiting space hotel from 2022, while Axiom Space and Bigelow Aerospace are also seeking to cash in on the anticipated increase of space tourists seeking accommodation.[13]

Meanwhile, the company SpaceX, owned by Elon Musk, is actively working towards establishing a colony on Mars. It is Musk's belief that the Earth will eventually become uninhabitable, so we should make preparations to leave it and become a 'multi-planetary species'.[14] He is not alone in holding such a view. The celebrated astrophysicist Stephen Hawking warned in 2017 that the human race must start leaving the Earth within 30 years to avoid being wiped out by over-population and climate change. He advocated the Moon and Mars as the best sites to begin the first colonies.[15] In 2018, a competition for designing a city on Mars inspired no less than 87,000 submissions, of which nearly 500 were deemed to have genuine potential to sustain meaningful life for a million humans. Both the competition itself, and the number of submissions, reveal the degree to which human beings are now in thrall to the fantasy of abandoning the Earth. It seems we are collectively losing the innate sense of belonging to our own planet.[16]

An Inner World That is Not Our Own

Given the rigours and expense of extraterrestrial flight, the provision of less arduous and cheaper ways of abandoning the Earth has been one of the gifts of the electronic age. It is surely a significant coincidence that the space programme began at more or less the same time as the era of television, which 'took off' during the 1950s. In 1949, only 2% of American households had television sets, but by 1954 this had risen to just under 60%.[17] NASA was founded in 1958, immediately commencing the

*Figure 2.1, The fantasy of abandoning the earth: the astronaut as the
new technological shaman.*

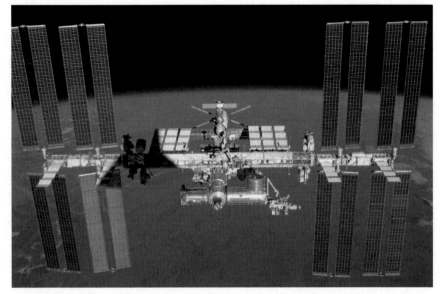

Figure 2.2, The International Space Station, providing accommodation for space tourists.

American manned space flight programme. This was in direct competition with the Soviet Union, which was at that time some way ahead of the USA. The first ever manned spaceflight was in 1961, when Yuri Gagarin completed a single orbit of the Earth. In the same year, 1961, 88% of the American population had at least one television set in their homes.[18] In other words, just as human beings lifted themselves beyond the Earth's atmosphere, so the desertion of the real world for the screen-mediated world began to reach epidemic proportions. In the 1960s, watching TV and going to the cinema rapidly became, after sleeping and working, the third largest use of time in the USA and Europe. In a remarkable series of photographs, taken in 1979 and entitled 'Movie Audience', the artist Jeff Wall portrays the hypnotic effect of film-watching on the audience. His photographs capture the way in which the soul is drawn out of itself to inhabit an inner world that is not its own (Fig. 2.3).

With the evolution of the Internet into a world-wide electronic information network in the mid-1990s, the pull away from the real world could only grow stronger. According to the Ofcom survey published in 2016, referred to in the previous chapter, while adults in the UK were spending on average over three hours a day online, they were spending an average of just under *nine hours per day* engaged with electronic media and communications technologies. That is more than the average amount of time people spend either sleeping or working. It is in fact more than half most people's waking hours.[19] These figures are set to rise as the Internet enters its next phase and frees itself from our computers and mobile devices and becomes embedded in the world, as an Internet of Things. Just as nature's ecosystems head towards catastrophic breakdown, an unprecedented effort

Figure 2.3, 'Movie Audience': inhabiting an inner world that is not our own by Jeff Wall.

is being expended in creating an 'electronic ecosystem' to support the new 'cyber-physical' reality that we are all increasingly required to inhabit. But the more human beings adjust to the cyber-world, the more their alienation from the natural world is accentuated.

We have already seen in the previous chapter how strong is the pull exercised by various interactive virtual technologies, from Augmented Reality applications to immersive experiences in virtual, computer-generated worlds entirely removed from one's immediate physical environment. It is interesting that the technology required for total immersion Virtual Reality was originally pioneered by none other than NASA in the 1980s. It involved what was then called a 'steroscopic head-mounted display' and 'data gloves' (Fig. 2.4).[20] That NASA's concerns extended beyond actual spaceflight to the development of technologies for entering virtual space seems peculiarly apt. So too is the fact that in 2020 one of the most advanced VR headsets and 'haptic vests', (which enable the user to experience virtual objects through the sense of touch, as well as through sight and sound) is named the 'Rapture Headset and Vest'.[21] The enormous popularity of immersive VR has made it into a multi-billion dollar industry, with the number of users climbing from 0.2 million in 2014 to more than 171 million users in 2018.[22] This points to a future in which illusory sensory experiences evoked through neuromuscular electrical stimulation,

Figure 2.4, Equipped with stereoscopic head-mounted display and data gloves, pioneered by NASA in the 1980s, human beings make ready to enter virtual space and exit real space.

and other means, will increasingly vie with real sensory experiences. Thus the conditions are prepared for people no longer to regard the natural world as the primary reality in which they live.[23]

Cosmic Agencies

Behind *The Hymn of the Pearl*, there is the tacit assumption that human history is enmeshed within the much vaster cosmic process of the outpouring of the divine into the world and the return of the divine to itself through humanity. From this wider perspective, what works into human history, as we pass through the different ages or *yugas*, does not have a simply human provenance. Insofar as human history is part of the cosmic saga of the self-realization of the divine, suprahuman agencies are also involved, both in a positive and in a negative or hindering way. In *The Hymn of the Pearl*, emphasis is placed on the figure of the opposing serpent, which in religious mythologies is often associated with binding humanity to the material world. But we also meet opposing powers in the heavenly realms. St Paul refers to them in his Letter to the Ephesians:

> For our struggle is not against flesh and blood, but against the rulers (*archai*), against the authorities (*exousiai*), against the powers of this world's darkness, and against the spiritual forces of evil in the heavenly realms.[24]

These 'spiritual forces of evil in the heavenly realms' could be understood as the forces opposed to the outflow of the divine into materiality, and whose will is set against the engagement of God in the material world.

Behind the human fantasy of abandoning the Earth, then, we may detect heavenly opposition to the incarnation of the human spirit in the flesh, which tirelessly seeks to divert us from fully dwelling on Earth. Rudolf Steiner identified this opposing power with the fallen archangel of Christian tradition, Lucifer.[25] There is a story about how this fiery being of light, along with the rebel angels who followed him, came to fall from heaven. It is told in one of the apocryphal texts of the Old Testament, called *The Life of Adam and Eve*, originally written in the early centuries of our era, and subsequently taken up in both Jewish and Islamic literary traditions, not least in the *Koran*.[26] It relates that when God first created Adam, he invited all the angels to come and bow down before his new creation, for God had instilled into Adam a spark of his own divine nature, and he was very pleased that he had been able to make a creature of the earth in his own divine image and likeness. All the angels came and bowed down before Adam. But one of them, identified in *The Life of Adam and Eve* only as the Devil (*diabolus*),

Figure 2.5, Iblis (on the left) refuses to bow before Adam.

proudly refused to bow before Adam, because Adam was a lower being, created after him. In the Koranic version, the fiery angel (referred to in the *Koran* as Iblis) refuses to prostrate himself before Adam, specifically because Adam is made of earth (Fig. 2.5).

The story suggests that it is the nature of this adversarial power to hold the earth in disdain, and thus to be opposed to the deeper purpose of the physical incarnation of the human spirit. Traditionally regarded as a regent of the air before his fall, Lucifer fails to understand that there could be any meaning in the divine involvement with the material world, and therefore he sets his will against it. Should we come to see the widespread tendency in contemporary culture to turn away from the Earth as stemming from a greater than human provenance, then the impulses and desires that live so strongly within the human psyche may be understood as part of a far bigger cosmological picture.

The Body as Machine

In *The Hymn of the Pearl*, we also meet the polar opposite tendency: the pull towards greater identification with matter, and thereby towards greater separation from the divine. Carried to an extreme, this would result in the intensification of the forces of contraction and compression that operate so strongly in *Kali Yuga,* to the point at which it becomes impossible for a return of the human spirit to its divine home to take place. In other words, far from *Kali Yuga* ending, it would intensify.

We meet this side of the polarity in the philosophy of scientific reductionism in which there is flintlike opposition to any view of the world that acknowledges the reality of the spirit. From seventeenth century mechanistic philosophers like Thomas Hobbes to mid-twentieth century scientists like Jacques Monod, and more recently Richard Dawkins, one detects an almost religious anti-religious fervour in their determination to prove that there is nothing more to life than physical processes. The desire to explain everything without recourse to God was one of the driving forces behind the scientific revolution, succinctly expressed by the eighteenth century mathematician and physicist Laplace when, in conversation with Napoleon, he is said to have declared that God was 'an unnecessary hypothesis'.[27] In the mechanistic philosophy of Descartes, Hobbes and others, which laid the foundations of the philosophical framework of the sciences, only mechanistic explanations were regarded as valid. And so the physical body came to be seen as a machine lacking any trace of ensoulment.

The view that the human body is just a machine has been one of the great rallying causes of scientific reductionism. For Monod, a Nobel prize-winning biochemist, 'The cell is a machine. The animal is a machine. Man is a machine.'[28] He would have us understand that the concept of life and of the living organism is an illusion: what is alive is in reality dead. The realm of life should therefore be approached with an engineer's expertise. Kevin Warwick, a distinguished British professor of engineering, has long argued that human beings are 'simply one type of machine, a biological, electrochemical form'.[29] After four hundred years of the dominance of mechanistic philosophy, by the second half of the twentieth century (when Warwick wrote these words) such opinions were no longer regarded as radical: they were simply expressing current scientific understanding.

I have a biology textbook written for children, published in 1990 under the title *The Human Machine.* The children for whom it was written are of course now well into their adulthood, many with children of their own. In the Introduction, the very first sentence reads, 'The human body is a fascinating and remarkable machine. Its design is far more complex than the most advanced computer...'[30] The author seeks to assure us that it is *only,* more complex'—it is still a machine, but just a more complex machine. Turn the pages and you see displayed the different joints in the human skeleton, pictured in the clean lines that one would find in any manual of basic engineering: pivot joint, hinge joint, ball and socket joint, etc. (Fig. 2.6). I wonder if those who were obliged to read this book when they were young remember it with affection, or now feel some degree of disquiet that this is what they were told before they were able to think for themselves.

If the body is a machine, then it can be treated as one would treat a machine. When parts wear out, then you simply replace them with new parts. 'Spare part' surgery has come to cover more and more body parts, from new hip joints and thighbones, to artery replacements and organ transplants. But the logical consequence of this view would be to replace the organic body altogether with a machine, if this could be shown to be more efficient, longer lasting and easier to maintain. This suggestion was already being made by various respected scientists during the twentieth century, like J. D. Bernal (the eminent physicist and historian of science) in the 1920s and Hans Moravec (professor of engineering at MIT) in the 1980s.[31]

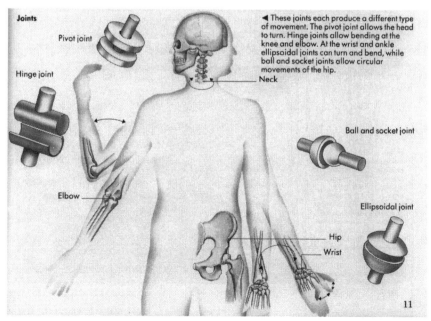

Figure 2.6, 'The human body is a fascinating and remarkable machine.' An illustration from a biology textbook for children (1990).

Soul and Spirit Denied

By the twentieth century, the extension of the machine metaphor to the brain could hardly be avoided. Whereas in the seventeenth century it was still felt necessary to reserve a place in the brain for the soul—as Descartes, for example, famously did—the deference to religious sensibilities simply could not be sustained as the scientific worldview took hold, displacing the previous religious worldview. By the twentieth century the soul, like God in the seventeenth century, had become an 'unnecessary hypothesis'. It is significant that early computer pioneers like Alan Turing and John von Neumann were convinced that the concepts of soul and spirit were redundant, and should be replaced by the physical brain. At the same time, they believed the brain would best be understood as an engineer would understand a computer, for computers are really machine-brains and hence provide the key to understanding how human brains work.[32]

The view that human consciousness is either a bi-product of complex brain-processes, or is no different from the brain-processes themselves, is now mainstream, along with the associated view that the brain is simply a neural computer. According to Steven Pinker,

> The mind is what the brain does; specifically, the brain processes information, and thinking is a kind of computation.[33]

It has become fashionable to talk about 'left brain' and 'right brain' thinking, as if logical thinking ('left brain') and intuitive, creative thinking ('right brain') are nothing more than brain functions, and it is the brain that is doing the thinking—not the person. It is a clear indication of how embedded the reductionist view has become that so many people are willing to adopt a way of speaking about the soul in terms that actually exclude it.

If the brain is regarded as just a 'neural computer', then certain consequences follow as to what is considered an appropriate way to treat it. The 'augmentation' of brain capacity by linking it to an actual computer, or other digital device, through electrode implants is one of these consequences. Indeed, there is a dreadful inevitability about it. As we saw in the last chapter, many decades of research have gone into the practicalities of creating a Brain Computer Interface. This is rapidly achieving a high level of sophistication. In 2019, Elon Musk's company, 'Neuralink', pioneered a procedure for implanting over 3000 electrodes in the brain to enable a wireless link-up of the brain with computers and other electronic devices, with the aim of producing a commercially viable Brain Computer Interface.[34] Neuralink is just one amongst many similar companies, in a crowded field, all intent on the same end.

A further consequence of this way of thinking, which has been taken up and developed especially in Transhumanist circles, is the idea of avoiding death through downloading the contents of the brain into a computer or some kind of computing subtratum. This idea, advocated for example by both Kevin Warwick and Ray Kurzweil, presupposes that our essential identity can be reduced to brain patterns that can be digitized and so not only digitally enhanced but also transferred across to a physical computing medium.[35] Thereby, both the biological body and the brain can be simultaneously 'upgraded'. But Kurzweil's vision of the future of humanity goes one step further. Convinced that we (and for that matter everything else in the world) are just 'data', he believes we shall ultimately transcend the need for physical instantiation in a body altogether. Our real identity lies in the 'software' of our brain patterns rather than in the 'hardware' of any physical computer or robot that might temporarily instantiate them. Our brain patterns are therefore independent of any individual computer circuitry.[36] And so we arrive at Kurzweil's idea of the future of humanity: we shall become infinitely expandable digital files, while our souls are reduced to electronic pulses.

One wonders how such a conception could appeal to any sane human being. Such thoughts express nothing but ignorance of and disgust towards nature, towards the living human organism, and the domain which specifically belongs to the life of the soul: emotion, feeling, and imagination. Gone too is the 'night world' of sleep and of dreams and of the spiritual impulse that comes to us from beyond the conscious mind.[37] At the same time this conception expresses a complete failure to understand the meaning and necessity of death, as the key that opens the way to the experience of the true meaning of immortality.

An Uncertain Outcome

Behind the drive to desacralize both body and mind, there is something more than simply human involved, for there is something more than simply human at stake. In terms of *The Hymn of the Pearl*, there is a pearl at stake, the symbol of the divine within ourselves and the world of nature to which we inherently belong. We need to recognize that the brilliant but unscrupulous intelligence we utilize to 'cyber-physicalize' nature, and to convince ourselves that the human soul and spirit are figments of an outmoded worldview, should be thought of not simply as originating within us, but as stemming from a greater than human power acting in the cosmos and within history. This power is the primary factor that carries the cosmic impulse toward separation from the divine. Humanity has had to submit to this impulse in order to become fully independent of the 'parental' world of its spiritual origins. Only then could there develop the possibility of a truly free return. But the impulse toward separation does not itself harbour any kindly undertow that would draw us back to the divine world of the Mother/ Father God. On the contrary, it is only to the extent that we succeed in overcoming it, as the prince succeeded in overcoming the serpent, that the return becomes possible.

If we were to personify this power, we would have to say that it seeks to drive out any residual awareness that God is present in nature, or that the human being is in any way capable of embodying divinity. Rather, it would lead us further and further from the spiritual world into a subnatural realm in which the inhuman prevails. William Blake characterized this power in two ways: in so far as it operates within human consciousness, it appears as the figure of Urizen—human intelligence bound within the 'single vision' of purely secular and rational thinking. But in its more cosmic aspect, Blake saw it as the being that in Christianity is referred to as Satan, who is distinguished from the fiery regent of the air, Lucifer, by his traditionally heavy and serpentine form. Rudolf Steiner identified this being with the ancient Persian god of darkness and sterility, Ahriman, the opponent of Ormuzd (or Ahura Mazda) the god of light.[38] In Blake's famous illustration, *Michael binding Satan* (Fig.2.7), Michael is portrayed as the representative of humanity, struggling as much to free himself from the power of the serpent as to bind it. Indeed, there is an ambivalence about who is binding who, and the outcome is by no means certain.

It is the opinion of some commentators that we are now in the very depths of *Kali Yuga*. In terms of *The Hymn of the Pearl*, we should still be waiting for the eagle to arrive and wake us from our slumbers. According to Steiner, however, we should understand that *Kali Yuga* has already ended. It ended before the twentieth century even began, in 1899.[39] If this doesn't seem probable given the many horrors of the twentieth century, the growing ascendancy of the inhuman in our midst and the environmental catastrophes that now threaten us, we may still accept that a new era is nevertheless struggling to be born. Or, to put it more exactly, something is struggling to be born in us—a consciousness of our true centre, the centre of spiritual intelligence and illumination within us—and it is this birth that will bring about a new era. We may think of it as the archetypal spirit-child, whose birth in many of the world's mythologies is met with the most

Figure 2.7, William Blake's depiction of the archangel Michael struggling as much to free himself from the Satanic power as to bind it.

intense opposition from the adversarial powers. In his essay on the child archetype, which carries with it all the promise of the new, Jung made the following comment:

> Nothing in all the world welcomes this new birth, although it is the most precious fruit of Mother Nature herself, the most pregnant with the future, signifying a higher stage of self-realization.[40]

Even if, as Steiner assures us, *Kali Yuga* really has ended, we should not therefore assume that this guarantees that the new age of light will automatically unfold. There is the possibility that, instead of the return to the divine, the momentum downwards will carry us even further away from the spiritual world.

We are living at a crucial period in the history of humanity, a period he described as humanity's biggest test.[41] Do we get ever more sucked into the materialist worldview, with its utilitarian ethic and its anti-human technology, or do we find a way forward and upward towards a more conscious co-operative working with the divine? If the latter, then both the 'Luciferic' temptation to make a wholly illusory return without the pearl, and the 'Ahrimanic' (or Satanic) temptation to live by the barren light of an intellect divorced from spiritual insight must be overcome. The impulse towards independence needs to be married with the buried yearning to return, just as the impulse to see our true destiny as lying beyond the world needs to be tempered by the recognition that there is a pearl to be won here on Earth.

In terms of *The Hymn of the Pearl*, we are no longer in the position of waiting for the eagle to appear, to rouse us and guide us towards our spiritual home. The fact is that many eagles appeared in the Western world during the twentieth century. We have had Jung and the foundation of depth psychology, we have had Steiner's renewal of the Western esoteric tradition and we have had the influx into the West of Buddhist philosophy and meditation practice. These are three major spiritual gifts, amongst others no less significant, that the twentieth century has passed on to us in the twenty-first century.[42] With so many wisdom traditions now available to us, it should be possible for everyone who genuinely seeks it, to find the spiritual guidance that they can resonate with. The onus is entirely on each one of us to wake up, to remember what we are here for, and to embark on the quest for the pearl.

On the urgency of our earnestly engaging in this quest, few have written more passionately and eloquently than the Sufi mystic and poet, Rumi, who wrote:

> There is one thing in this world which you must never forget to do. If you forget everything else and not this, there's nothing to worry about, but if you remember everything else and forget this, then you will have done nothing with your life.

> It's as if a king has sent you to some country to do a task, and you perform a hundred other services, but not the one he sent you to do. And not doing it is like using a priceless Indian sword to slice rotten meat, or like cooking turnips in a golden bowl, or like thrusting the finest tempered knife into a wall so you can hang things from it.

> You may say, 'But look, I'm using the knife. It is not lying idle.' Do you hear how ludicrous that sounds? Any old iron nail could be used for the same

purpose. You may say, 'But I spend my energies on lofty pursuits. I study Law and Philosophy and Astronomy and Medicine and all the rest'. But consider why you do those things. They are all branches of yourself.

Remember the deep root of your being, the inner presence of God. Give your life to the one who already owns your breath and your every moment. If you don't, you will be exactly like the person who hammers a precious knife into the kitchen wall and uses it for a peg on which to hang some pot. You will be wasting the keenness of your life and foolishly ignoring your true dignity and your purpose. [43]

Chapter Three

THE ADVENT OF THE WEARABLE COMPUTER

The Smartwatch

When, in January 2013, the first of a new generation of smartwatches became available to the public, it was an instant success. The 'Pebble' smartwatch achieved sales of 300,000 in its first year, rising to a million by the end of the following year.[1] Worn on the wrist like a normal watch, it connected wirelessly (via Bluetooth) to the wearer's smartphone, allowing them to identify callers, read text messages and emails, switch songs on their iPhone, view weather alerts and various other features that we have come to expect of smartwatches (Fig.3.1). Although earlier generations of smartwatches had already appeared in the 1980s, and then again in the 1990s, in both cases production had been abandoned after a few years because of lack of uptake.[2] But an unprecedented buzz of excitement gathered around Pebble, as if at last the moment had finally come for the smartwatch to establish itself in our daily lives. As it turned out, the Pebble smartwatch met a similar fate to its predecessors, and the company filed for insolvency at the end of 2016. Nevertheless, it did inaugurate the new era of the wearable computer.

One of the reasons for the demise of the Pebble smartwatch was that in 2015, two years after its launch, Apple released a rival smartwatch, the 'Apple Watch', as if in response to the same intuition that had inspired Pebble: namely, that *the time had come* for computers to become wearable. Both companies had their fingers on the pulse of where the Digital Revolution was heading next, sensing that we were on the brink of a new phase in our relationship to electronic technology. Alan Dye, the man responsible for overseeing the design of the user interface of the Apple Watch described how the concept of the Apple Watch emerged:

> There was a sense that technology was going to move onto the body. We felt like the natural place, the place that had historical relevance and significance, was the wrist.[3]

Initially, the purpose of the Apple Watch was not immediately apparent to the team who were working on its design. They were feeling it out

Figure 3.1, The Pebble Smartwatch.

as they went along, following an intuition that computer technology was heading towards adapting itself to the body.[4] What lacked sufficient appeal in the 1980s and 1990s would, they believed, be embraced in the second decade of the twenty-first century. And they were proved right. Since its launch in 2015, each year the Apple Watch gets an upgrade, having established its position in the now crowded market for smartwatches.

Along with the smartwatch, the second decade of the twenty-first century saw the rapid growth in dedicated wearable fitness trackers that monitor the wearer's heart rate, number of steps taken, calories used, and so on. One of the best known, Fitbit, saw its sales rise from a mere 60,000 devices in 2010 to over 10 million by 2014, rising to over 22 million by 2016.[5] At the end of that year, when Pebble filed for insolvency, Fitbit acquired its assets and subsequently went into the production of smartwatches, with the now standard features of notification of messages, music control, the ability to make payments from the wrist, etc., along with advanced fitness tracking capabilities. The huge and growing popularity of such wearable devices has led to the market becoming flooded with offerings from a large number of different companies.

While of course this surge in popularity of smartwatches could be put down simply to the usefulness of the range of functions they offer, something deeper is at work as well, which reflects our changing relationship with technology. Certainly, the trajectory of the development of digital technologies has been towards miniaturization, and this has enabled the design of devices that afford greater intimacy between them and us. But we have also to recognize that human beings have grown more comfortable with their digital devices, and are actively seeking a closer connection with them. There is a hunger for this, and the hunger is felt by many as an inner need. What is it that lies behind this desire to become more closely integrated with computers? What is the promise that closer integration offers? Before attempting to answer this question, we must turn to a development that paralleled that of the smartwatch.

Smart Glasses

About the same time as the Pebble team launched their pioneering smartwatch, another wearable computer project also drew a lot of attention, based on sensational promotional videos. This was the Google Glass project—a bold attempt to create what was essentially a wearable smartphone in the form of 'smart glasses', with the capacity to display information in front of the wearer's eyes without it blocking the field of vision (Fig.3.2). The glasses enabled the wearer to access content from the Internet, send text messages, take photos, and download and run a range of apps. They could be controlled through voice command as well as through a touchpad on one arm of the glasses. After a somewhat bumpy ride, Google Glass continues to offer new and improved designs, with the sales emphasis being towards industry. The sales pitch for the updated 'Enterprise Edition' is that smartglasses help workers to be more efficient, by overlaying virtual content in the form of information, instructions or visual data on the wearer's perception of the real environment.[6] They effectively create the perceptual experience of a hybrid reality, both physical and virtual at the same time. This hybrid reality, referred to as Augmented Reality, arises out of the enmeshing of computer generated content with normal sensory experience, so that a further element is introduced to our perception of the world.

It is important to understand that this third, computer-generated element arises neither from the world we naturally perceive, nor from our inner life of thought and feeling which normally bestows meaning on our perceptions. It is an extraneous input that is delivered by the technology. In Figure 3.3, one of the first farming apps for Google Glass (called Intelli-Scout) offers farmers a corn kernel count. All the farmer has to do is slowly rotate a corn cob in front of his smartglasses, and they then provide him with the data (Fig.3.3).

Figure 3.2, Google Glass face-mounted wearable computer.

Figure 3.3, Deflected from the real to the virtual cob.

In this example, we see how, through becoming wearable, the computer comes to assume a pivotal role in both our sense perceptions and our thought processes, encouraging us to defer to the electronic interface and the bottomless reservoir of information that can instantly be summoned up and placed between our direct sensory experience and our inner life of thought, feeling and decision. It makes us feel more powerful, more in control, but the kind of empowerment it offers is what Heidegger called the rule of *Gestell* or 'enframing'—fixing things in a framework of meaning that is entirely instrumental to our purposes (see Chapter One, p.10). Because our attention is drawn away from the immediate perception of the phenomenon in front of us to the virtual content interposed between it and us, our relationship to it becomes secondary to our relationship to the data that it has been reduced to. As a result, our thought processes are steered away from 'being present' to its intrinsic qualities, towards a purely utilitarian relationship. Any deeper engagement is thwarted, not just by the particular program that we may be using, but by the technology itself which, while it purports to ease our relationship to the world, actually alienates us even further from it. If wearing smartglasses became habitual, we would be constantly diverted from direct encounter with the world to its virtual re-presentation as a data stream, set of instructions or whatever else the app superimposes on it. We would be humanly diminished because we would become trapped in a purely instrumental mindset that treats everything as a means to achieving our pre-established ends.

Since the launch of Google Glass, other companies have produced a large number of different brands of smartglasses, with much effort being put into designs that will appeal to the most fashion-conscious consumer, while also providing a total overlay of the visual field. Michael Abrash, chief scientist of Oculus VR (acquired by Facebook in 2014), has no doubt that smartglasses will eventually replace smartphones altogether. Speaking in 2017, he said:

> Twenty or thirty years from now, I predict that instead of carrying stylish smartphones everywhere, we'll wear stylish glasses. Those glasses will offer VR, AR and everything in between and we'll use them all day.[7]

While the main capabilities of smartglasses at present remain those of a wearable iPhone, with the ability to interpose a layer of digital content of one sort or another (graphics, measurements, words, audio content and images) on what we perceive in the world, in time this will change in various ways. First of all, hand and voice control will be replaced by mind control, through combining the smartglasses with a headset. As we saw in the previous chapter (p.42), technology has advanced a long way towards being able to offer this capability. Secondly, tech companies have been developing the ability to go beyond a mere information overlay to the creation of illusory three dimensional entities in physical space, so virtual objects can become located in the physical world. The result is what is called Mixed Reality, in which virtual objects and entities appear to have volume, density and substance, and can be made to behave just as if they were physically real.

A company called Magic Leap (in which Google and other tech companies have invested hundreds of millions of dollars) has been working on smartglasses that perfect the experience of Mixed Reality. Referred to as 'spatial computing', it lies on the other side of the Internet of Things, insofar as the virtual claims a kind of existential equality with the real. Rony Abovitz, the founder of Magic Leap, believes that Mixed Reality will be *the reality* for a large number of human beings in the future:

> So our goal is to ultimately build spatial computing into something that a lot of people in the world can use all day every day all the time everywhere. [8]

In other words, the aim is to transform the reality in which human beings live by enabling non-physical, computer-generated entities to be experienced as part of our physical world, while at the same time having the possibility of our inhabiting non-physical, computer-generated virtual worlds.

One of the things spatial computing makes possible is so-called 'telepresence', when someone can not only give the appearance of being present in a distant physical location, but also feel they *are* present (as they do when entering a virtual world by wearing a VR headset).[9] Thereby real and computer-generated spaces can become interchangeable: human beings will become accustomed to existing in both. One company working towards telepresence is Microsoft, with its 'Hololens' series of smartglasses. These map the room a person is in so as to be able to introduce interactive holograms into their physical environment. This includes 'holoportation', which would allow participants in remote locations to be present in each other's physical reality.[10] Another company is Innovega, which will soon introduce its 'eMacula' smartglasses and contact lens combination, which at the time of writing are not yet commercially available. Innovega explicitly seeks to go beyond 'the flat and lifeless screen of a smartphone or tablet' in order to 'merge the digital and real world, providing an uncompromising augmented and mixed reality experience'.[11] Innovega worked closely with the US military (who initially provided the company with much of its funding) to produce something light-weight but with high definition images, offering a panoramic (up to 100°) field of view. In the eMacula Vision Statement, we read:

> We believe the world is ready for a new human friendly digital interface without any trade-offs....We want the virtual and real world to merge seamlessly.[12]

The impression one has, in contemplating these developments, is that what is being prepared are new conditions of life in which our relationship to nature is thrust into the background by the increasing dominance of the virtual, while our relationship to our own inner world is subverted by the constant intrusion of extraneous virtual content that draws us away from the experience of our own soul-space. Already, Virtual Reality vies with real reality for people's attention and loyalty, but when it eventually accommodates itself within the physical world of our daily experience, then it would even more effectively compete with any deeper inclination that we might have to dwell more intimately with nature, and equally to come back to ourselves, to the stillness at the heart of the inner life. It thus presents humanity with an enormous challenge. As we have seen in the Introduction, the world's spiritual traditions have been the guardians of what it means to be human, and the Western monastic tradition in particular has always emphasized the importance both of cultivating a contemplative, reverential relationship to nature, and the meditative practice of stilling the mind, bringing it back to its own centre. It is precisely to such contemplative ends that much wise guidance has been devoted, for even under favourable conditions these ends are not easy to attain. Whatever benefits spatial computing may have to offer, they would seem to lie in the opposite direction of that to which the path of contemplation leads.

It could be argued that smartglasses can always be taken off, or turned off, but this would require that the wearer is strong-willed enough to break the habit of constantly wearing them. Furthermore, it is important to note that Innovega's smartglasses/contact lens combination should be seen as an intermediate 'hybrid' on the way to something far more advanced. The longer-term aim, whose realization is still some years away, is to develop a stand-alone contact lens, without the need to work in conjunction with glasses (see Chapter One, pp.22-23). But even that is not the endpoint. According to Innovega's CEO, Steve Willey, the ultimate goal is to develop a lens that could be implanted into the eye and 'hardwired' permanently.[13] Then the question of what ultimately it means to be human once again confronts us. Through the eye, the human soul engages with the world. If the eye through which the soul engages is permanently hardwired, so that what appears before it is electronically mediated, this will effectively draw a curtain across the window of the soul. And then we must expect the more delicate faculties of the soul to shrivel up for lack of light; for the light that we draw on for illumination of the inner life is precisely the light that the electronic interface shuts out.

The Internet of Things

But let us backtrack to the more immediate future. In order for smartglasses to be able meaningfully to overlay and thus usefully 'augment' the physical reality we perceive, it is necessary for what we perceive in the world to be computer-compatible and, from a digital point of view, information rich. The inexorable advance towards wearable and finally, biologically integral, computing, with the opportunities this will give for melding virtual and physical realities into a relatively seamless experience is to a large extent dependent upon the migration of the Internet itself, from computers functioning in an interconnected but self-enclosed computer network, to a network that *includes the physical environment* and physical objects in this environment. To this end, the whole world is rapidly being incorporated into a vast electronic information system, the so-called 'Internet of Things'.

The decade in which smartwatches and smartglasses entered the marketplace was also the decade in which large IT companies, including IBM, Microsoft, and Advantech, committed themselves to the massive expansion of the number of 'intelligent' computer devices embedded in the environment. Their ambition was quite breathtaking. It was to capture the whole planet in an information technology web, an all-encompassing electronic infrastructure that would make the planet 'intelligent' (Fig.3.4). For many years now, the physical objects that surround us have been fast acquiring transmitters and receivers, micro-sensors and actuators that have been binding things into computer networks. To give one small but familiar example, think of the popularity of the Global Positioning System, or 'sat nav', that binds your car into just such a global network.

One company involved in the project to make the planet 'smart' is HP Labs (the HP stands for Hewlett Packard). In 2012, it described its goal as being to implement 'a new information ecosystem, the Central Nervous System for the Earth (CeNSE), consisting of a trillion nanoscale sensors and actuators embedded in the environment and connected via an array of networks with computing systems, software and services.' The stated aim of HP Labs was to 'revolutionize human interaction with the earth as profoundly as the Internet has revolutionized personal and business interactions.'[14] The statement signals the commencement of a deeper stage in the ongoing Digital Revolution, a stage that takes aim at our most fundamental relationship: our relationship to the Earth.

Figure 3.4, Enabling an artificially 'intelligent' planet. (Publicity image from Advantech's website, 2012).

We are now witnessing the transformation of both our urban and our natural environments from a condition of technological innocence to one in which they are electronically despoiled as they are tied into the ever more sophisticated 'information ecosystem'. A rapidly increasing number of digital devices are being embedded in the world of physical things, with Wireless Sensor Networks (WSN) detecting and measuring diverse physical conditions in order to give us greater control of our environments; and the deployment of technologies for endowing more and more things with electronic identities. One crucial component for accomplishing the latter is what is known as Automatic Identification and Data Capture (AIDC) technology, which ranges from simple barcodes to more complex facial recognition technology. The ubiquitous RFID (Radio Frequency Identification) chip or tag falls under this category. It has an integrated circuit for storing information, and can both send and receive an encoded radio signal that can be accessed at a distance, even if the tag itself is not physically visible because of intervening objects. With more and more things and creatures (no doubt eventually including human beings) equipped with these miniscule identifying devices, from cows in the field to leather boots in the shops, from buildings and automobile parts on the assembly line to the pet cat or dog injected with an RFID chip, less and less will escape the electronic information net that is being cast over the world.[15] Equipped with wearable computing devices, and armed with the appropriate dedicated software programmes, those who wear them will be able to lay claim to information about objects, creatures and perhaps other people in their immediate environment, otherwise inaccessible to those who are not so equipped. This is not because they will have developed a personal relationship to them, or a greater insight into them, or love or understanding of them, but because their wearable computer will have given them the power to access relevant information held on an electronic database. Here, then, we see the way in which the electronic information ecosystem can revolutionize human interaction with the earth and all living creatures, as well as inevitably altering the social and political climate in which we live.

Another important aspect of the data-capture project central to the Internet of Things is to make the appliances that we use on a daily basis 'smart', from toothbrushes to fridges, from hairbrushes to mattresses. Being smart means that they are constantly collecting data and feeding it back not only to us but also to other interested parties, such as the company that made them, and various third-party companies that we may or may not have given our permission to harvest our data. In June 2018, *Which?* magazine published a report on data collection from household smart appliances and found more than 20 other companies (including marketing companies) in addition to the manufacturers on the receiving end of data transfers from some devices. It also found televisions selling viewing data to advertisers, toothbrushes with access to smartphone microphones, and security cameras that could be hacked to let outsiders watch and listen to people in their own homes.[16] When things become smart, they become a source of data that many third parties will seek out, and might acquire with or without your consent. When a home becomes smart, it opens your private life to surveillance, all the more so if you are also wearing a smartwatch or smartglasses, which also feed back data to the company that sold them to you. As Shoshana Zuboff has explained, we have now entered the era of 'surveillance capitalism', closely aligned with surveillance politics.[17] The Internet of Things is at the very heart of it.

For this reason, we should not for a moment assume that the Internet of Things is ever going to be a docile servant of humanity. Not only does it enable information to be released *to* the human being, but also *from* the human being to a predatory world of economic and political interests. As Zuboff says:

> Nearly every product or service that begins with the word 'smart' or 'personalized', every internet-enabled device, every 'digital assistant', is simply a supply-chain interface for the unobstructed flow of behavioural data on its way to predicting our futures in a surveillance economy.[18]

It might be argued that this does not have any impact on our inherent freedom to make decisions and choices based on our own thoughts, judgements and desires. But the more data that is collected from us, the more susceptible do our thoughts, judgements and desires become to being manipulated by those who seek to profit from us or control us. Then the technology becomes the battleground for human freedom, for it works constantly and shamelessly to undermine it. For example, the data analytics company Cambridge Analytica was able to use Facebook profiles for blatant political ends during the 2016 UK referendum on EU membership.[19] In the public arena, the combination of CCTV, biometrics, facial recognition technology and tracking technologies is a powerful instrument of control when combined with comprehensive databases. But in the private arena of our homes and domestic lives, smart appliances are a Trojan horse for surveillance capitalists and governments, which we invite into our homes at our peril. They complete the infrastructure of electronic totalitarianism that is wide open to misuse and abuse from both corporate interests and from those who rule us.

The exponentially increasing degree of surveillance, however, is not the only aspect of this next stage of the Digital Revolution that should be of concern. As the new electronic infrastructure roots itself in our lives, and as the Earth acquires its digital 'Central Nervous System', we should also be aware of a further significant danger that the advent of the wearable computer entails.

The Electrification of the Air

One of the prerequisites of the widespread adoption of wearable computers is the saturation of the atmosphere with electromagnetic radiation, at intensities far beyond anything that could possibly be described as natural. The defining ambition of the 5G electronic information network is that mobile computing should be fully functional anywhere and at anytime, wherever you are on the planet.[20] This requires that the whole globe be permanently bathed in high density electromagnetic fields.

While electromagnetic fields have their place in nature, they are extremely weak compared to the electromagnetic fields artificially propagated by the communications industry. According to Ulrich Warnke, of the University of Saarland in Germany.

> Technical wireless communication such as mobile radio, radio, TV and satellite communication is only possible because the power density of the utilized technical high frequency spectrum far exceeds that of natural radiation.[21]

'Far exceeds' is something of an understatement. It has been estimated that in urban areas the average ambient power density of radiofrequency radiation is one thousand billion times (i.e. one followed by twelve zeros) the natural background levels. Another estimate puts the figure for frequencies in the 1 GHz band at *ten billion billion* times (ten followed by eighteen zeros) greater than natural levels.[22] To make any sense of such figures is almost impossible. It is hard enough to imagine what a hundred times greater than natural levels might mean, let alone ten billion billion! But, if nothing else, it signals the need for us to wake up to the possible consequences that such high exposure levels might have. Our natural environment and all the creatures that are part of it, including of course ourselves, are now obliged to live within an atmosphere that has, beginning with the first radio wave broadcasts in the 1920s, become radically altered from how it used to be before radio and wireless communication began. If it is now permeated with a diverse range of high frequency radio waves, which exceed natural levels of electromagnetic radiation by a factor that is unimaginably high, then why should we assume that this is perfectly harmless and is not going to have an adverse effect on us and other living organisms—especially when so much evidence points to the existence of just such effects?[23]

Radio waves are sometimes euphemistically called 'air waves', since they travel through the air. But they are not actually *air* waves: they are waves of radiant electricity, which—like the air—we cannot see, hear, smell, taste or touch. We know the air is there because we breathe it in and out, and our lives utterly depend on it from moment to moment. But we are inclined to forget that our clever wireless devices can only be so clever because every time they link us to the Internet or allow us to make a call, they are 'inhaling' and 'exhaling' an electrified atmosphere that we have artificially engendered for them. Both wireless computing and the creation of the 'Central Nervous System for the Earth' require the maintenance and enhancement of this electrified atmosphere. The United Kingdom, like every other country in the world, is under constant pressure to 'improve' its wireless communication infrastructure, so that the atmosphere is ever more densely saturated with electromagnetic radiation. The 4G spectrum introduced in the UK in 2013 was favoured because it was supposed to be particularly good at penetrating forests and traversing hills, as well as having six times the speed of 3G, enabling it to handle much more complex data streams and more sophisticated software applications.[24] The rollout of 5G, which began in the UK in 2019, will not replace 4G, but supplement it with more frequency bands, including utilization of much higher frequencies with wavelengths in the millimetre range, so as to ensure even greater bandwidth and increased data flow.[25] As the wireless communication network becomes ever more complex and multi-layered, the degree of electromagnetic pollution to which natural ecosystems and living organisms are subjected only rises.

Over the last 50 years, a very large number of scientific studies have been conducted that demonstrate beyond reasonable doubt that the radio frequency radiation issuing from the network of transmission masts, satellites, routers, and so on, which our mobile devices need in order to work—as well as from the devices themselves—have a detrimental effect on living creatures: plant, insect, bird, amphibian, mammal and human.[26] Without going into the complex physical mechanisms involved, one of the principal impacts (but by no means the only one) of this radiation is that it disrupts the circadian rhythms of living organisms, thereby weakening their immune systems.[27] A great deal of the available research indicates that electromagnetic radiation is inimical to life, because the formative, life-giving forces (i.e. the etheric body) of living organisms are intimately connected to their circadian rhythms.[28] Long before any of this evidence was available, Rudolf Steiner, speaking from his own spiritual researches, made a number of statements concerning the nature of electricity and specifically its relationship to the etheric realm, (or life-realm). In a question and answer session after a lecture given in 1924, he said:

> Electricity, once and for all, is not intended to work into the realm of the living—it is not meant to help living things especially; it cannot do so. You must know that electricity is at a lower level than that of living things. Whatever is alive—the higher it is, the more it will tend to ward off electricity. It is a definite repulsion.[29]

The antipathy that Steiner perceived as characterizing the relationship of electricity to living organisms does not mean that living organisms cannot and do not utilize electricity. It is well known that electricity is present within living organisms at the cellular level and is employed in communicating signals from one part of the body to another. But within the living organism, as in the natural environment, electrical activity is in minute, almost homeo-pathic potencies, with electrical potentials measured in single or double-figure milli-volts, and electric currents measured in the tiniest possible strength of pico-amps. Thereby it is rendered subservient to the energies of life. When confronted by vastly more powerful, raw electrical forces, often in complex interrelationships with each other, oscillating at different fre-quencies, from multi-directional sources (especially in urban environments), and pulsed because carrying digital information, it is not surprising that the immune systems of plants, animals and humans suffer, and they become more susceptible to disease.

It is also of particular relevance that Steiner in the same lecture as the one referred to above, which was given just one year after the first national radio broadcasts commenced in Germany, singled out radiant electricity as affecting the ability of human beings to think, dampening down human intelligence.[30] Loss of memory, poor concentration, reduced attention spans and reduced cognitive function are all effects that have consistently been associated with exposure to radio frequency radiation, as has Alzheimer's Disease.[31] This, it would appear, is the price being exacted from human beings for the establishment of an electromagnetically based 'Central Ner-vous System for the Earth'.

The Singularity

It might seem that the driving forces behind the advent of the wearable computer, the Internet of Things and the increasingly dense 'electrosmog' that is making the atmosphere in which we live ever more hostile to health, are to be located on the one hand in the seemingly insatiable consumer demand for new technologies, and on the other hand in the enormous prof-its to be made by the IT companies and governments who cater to (and to a large extent generate) this demand. While these are certainly powerful fac-tors, I have suggested in the previous chapter that there are other forces, of which we are for the most part unconscious or only semi-conscious, which also play a decisive role. One of the ways in which we can become more conscious of these forces is by turning our attention to the final destination towards which current technological developments are taking us, for these forces work into the present from the future.

At the beginning of this chapter I referred to the way in which the design of the Apple Watch emerged, without the designers having any clear conception of its purpose but guided by an inner sense that the time had come for computers to become wearable. The design team were aware that the direction of travel was towards technology moving onto the body, but they were not initially aware of the purposes this would serve.[32] This example points to the fact that the Digital Revolution has a direction of travel that is steering research agendas and investment decisions, but it is towards a future that most of us—including some of those who are driving it forward—but dimly conceive. The outpouring of new electronic products and devices doesn't happen by itself. Behind it are human beings who have ideas and inspirations, but they are not aware of the source from which these ideas and inspirations come, nor do they reflect deeply on the consequences of realizing them. Thus human beings are drawn into the service of powers whose existence they know nothing of, and human ingenuity is harnessed and human desires are stirred up, so as to bend both to the realization of aims that may or may not serve our true spiritual interests.

A number of contemporary thinkers subscribing to the technophile ideology of Transhumanism, for example Ray Kurzweil in the USA, Yuval Noah Harari in Israel, and Nick Bostrom in the United Kingdom, have however given us an extremely clear picture of where such developments as the advent of the wearable computer and the Internet of Things actually belong in a wider teleological (or goal-oriented) perspective.[33] If we consider Kurzweil's nightmare predictions in his book, *The Singularity is Near*, we find them presented on a timescale that leads us, blow by blow, to an event in the middle of this century (to be precise, 2045), which he calls the 'Singularity'. Kurzweil defines the Singularity as:

> the culmination of the merger of our biological thinking and existence with our technology, resulting in a world that is still human but that transcends our biological roots. There will be no distinction, post-Singularity, between human and machine or between physical and virtual reality.[34]

According to Kurzweil, by mid-century, machine intelligence (i.e. computational power, measured in the number of operations per second) will be trillions of times greater than it is today, and the pressure on us to merge with this exponentially increasing machine intelligence through neural implants will be irresistible over the coming years.

The advent of the wearable computer, in this vision of things, is the next incremental step towards the union of machines and human beings, bringing us closer both to the integration of computer technology within the physical organism, and to a coalescence of virtual and real worlds in our daily experience. While the next generation of smartglasses may seem to many as the coolest innovation yet, they will soon enough be outmoded, and not just by smart contact lenses, or subsequently by retinal implants. By the 2030s, according to Kurzweil, nanotechnology will have advanced far enough to enable tiny nano-machines to be directly inserted into the brain, enabling people to switch from normal sensory perception of the environment to full-immersion Virtual Reality without the need for any other external intervention.[35]

Just as Transhumanist ideology envisages the human future as inseparable from the machine, so too it envisages nature's destiny as to serve as a kind of substratum of a vast artificial Global Brain. What the Internet of Things, and the creation of a so-called 'intelligent planet', means is the total saturation of the Earth with non-biological 'intelligence'. Through emerging nanotechnologies and enhanced microelectronics, 'intelligent' control of the natural environment and many of the organisms within it will be greatly strengthened. And so the Global Brain awakens. Kurzweil devotes a whole chapter to what will happen beyond this point, and produces the dizzying vision of Artificial Intelligence eventually radiating out from our electronically enhanced Earth and saturating the whole universe. Thus the destiny of the universe is conceived as being ultimately to become an enormous supercomputer.[36] It is a dream of insane proportions, but precisely in this aspect of Kurzweil's thinking are we able to catch sight of the cosmic (and diabolical) source of its inspiration, and the hatred of living nature that fuels it.

Despite the nightmarish character of Kurzweil's vision of humanity's future evolution, his book *The Singularity is Near* has received support from a number of significant figures, including Bill Gates and various other prominent persons in the IT world.[37] Not only that, but in 2009, Kurzweil co-founded a high-profile research and teaching institute in Silicon Valley, appropriately named 'Singularity University'. Backed by Google, NASA, and various other big names, its mission is to train a new global elite to work with emerging technologies and, as its name indicates, to prepare for the mid-century merger of humans and machines on the one hand, and real and virtual realities on the other. In Singularity University major global problems are addressed, such as how to feed the world, how to clean up pollution, etc. on the premise that all problems (big and small) can find technological solutions by 'simple methods combined with heavy doses of computation.'[38] While we may recognize in this focus on current world problems a thin thread of idealism at work within the Transhumanist/Singularitarian movement, the tenor of thought is unremittingly technocentric and anthropocentric, the Earth being viewed merely as the backdrop for human 'enhancement'. But due to the reduced conception of the human being as essentially a biological computer, the notion of human enhancement is limited to enhanced *computational* power: it does not rise beyond cleverness to anything approaching wisdom, spiritual insight or genuine self-actualization. The goal of humanity is conceived as being to become more and more clever, as if this were the equivalent of becoming spiritually fulfilled. But becoming more and more clever through increased computational power belongs, of course, to the evolution of intelligent machines. This is why, to those who adhere to this view that humans are biological computers, like for example Stephen Hawking, the merger with artificial machine intelligence appears to be the only way forward for future human evolution, in order to avoid our being overtaken by ever more clever machines.[39]

Kurzweil's writings and the Singularity University programme are just two pointers to the fact that current technological developments are not taking place in an ideological vacuum, but within a highly materialistic philosophical matrix, which is unable to conceive of a deeper level of thinking than that which solves problems through computational power alone. This is in the tradition of Bacon, Hobbes, Descartes and Leibniz, whose mission it was to replace spiritual contemplation with calculative thinking as the paradigm for gaining knowledge. The history of modern computer technology has its origins in the mechanistic philosophy form-ulated in the seventeenth century by these thinkers.[40] Along with the thor-oughly materialistic assumptions of this stream of philosophy, this type of thinking continues to underpin the research that is conducted today and the long-term goals that are set for future innovations. No matter if many of those who use these technologies have a developed inner spiritual life, and would be the last to condone the materialistic worldview, the technol-ogies themselves are not philosophically neutral. Computer technology as such is an embodiment of reductionist thinking.[41]

The Challenges We Face

The advent of the wearable computer presents us all with the challenge as to how far and how warmly we are prepared to extend our embrace of digital technology, as we move towards the projected merger of human and machine. Let us suppose that in the next decade smartglasses become as pop-ular as smartphones are today. Knowing that this is another incremental step towards the eventual biological integration of computer technology, would you be prepared to take a stand and say, 'This is far enough. I will not wear smartglasses'? Or would you be inclined to think that, because we can take the smartglasses off, this still falls short of biological integration, and so is acceptable? Here is a choice that we all are likely to have to make very soon.

But as the evidence mounts that radio frequency and microwave radiation are killing trees in urban environments, are a major contributing factor to the collapse of bee colonies, are a cause of the decline in sparrows as well as affecting the breeding success of other birds, induce deformities in amphibians and cancer in rodents, and so on and on, not to mention making life on the planet intolerable for the roughly 3% or more of the population who suffer from electro-hypersensitivity, should we not also question our use of WiFi and smartphones too? [42] This is a moral question that is going to intensify as, over the coming years, research results into the negative effects of electromagnetic fields on living organisms become more incontrovertible and, hopefully, better publicized.

There is yet another, more formidable challenge, however, which runs alongside this moral question. And this is the challenge of addressing the hunger that humanity feels so strongly for greater connection with the realm of spirit, and which many mistakenly seek to satisfy through greater connection with technology. For the strength of the enticement of the virtual world may best be understood as being due to its offering an alluring counterfeit to the genuine spiritual experiences that alone can satisfy this spiritual hunger. Here we have to face a different kind of choice, which concerns our responsibility to care for ourselves. Are we prepared to take in hand the difficult task of inner development, as a conscious decision, followed through in daily practice? It seems to me that only when we do this can we stand a chance of coming into the right human relationship with our technologies. Whatever is happening at a collective level, we still have the freedom as individuals to make choices and embark on resolves. At the very least, we can designate times and places that are technology-free: not to use it on Sundays, for example, and to have one room in the house that is free of it—small steps to conserve our souls. Given its addictive nature, the technology actually presents an opportunity for us, by resisting it, to lift the veil on what it is concealing from us, and to glimpse that greater, more authentic experience from which it continually diverts us.

In Plato's *Republic*, the philosopher describes a threshold experience of fundamental importance in human life. He calls it the 'inner turn', or *metastrophê*, of the soul toward the realm of spirit.[43] It leads to our developing an interior faculty of knowing, through opening the 'eye' of the soul, so that it becomes capable of perceiving realities invisible to the physical eye. The 'inner turn' is an experience familiar to many spiritual traditions, and is often preceded by a powerful 'call' to an individual to awaken from the unreflective consciousness in which he or she is immersed. The challenge to make this 'inner turn' has never been easy to meet, the 'call' often hard to heed. And perhaps it has never been more difficult than it is today, with the countless pressures and distractions with which we daily have to contend. Perhaps, though, on a collective level, the very power of enthralment that our technologies wield over us needs to be recognized as masking that deeper call to the soul to make the inner turn. In which case, before smartglasses flood the market and we become yet more entranced by the false promise of virtuality, now seems like a good time to attend to the opening of the inner eye.

Chapter Four

5G: THE MULTIPLE ASSAULT

5G from Space

In 2018, the United States Federal Communications Commission (FCC) authorized the rocket company SpaceX, owned by the entrepreneur Elon Musk, to launch two satellite fleets to provide global satellite broadband services to every corner of the Earth. The first fleet would consist of 4,425 satellites. Essentially orbiting phone masts, they would use phased array, beam-forming systems to transmit and receive signals to and from the Earth at a height of approximately 750 miles, with transmission frequencies of between 10 GHz and 30 GHz.[1] The second fleet would consist of 7,518 satellites operating at a height of approximately 210 miles, and would transmit at somewhat higher frequencies of between 37.5 GHz and 42 GHz.[2] The project was christened 'Starlink', and it was envisaged in 2018 that the grand total of just under 12,000 satellites would be sufficient to cover all exigencies. But in October 2019, SpaceX surprised many observers by submitting further proposals for an additional 30,000 satellites, to be deployed at some unspecified time in the future.[3]

In order to put the scale of these proposals in perspective, in 2018 there were in total approximately two thousand fully functioning satellites orbiting the Earth. Some beamed down commercial GPS (or 'SatNav'), some provided TV, some provided smartphone services, and some produced high definition images for meteorologists and military surveillance. In addition to these actively functioning satellites there were roughly three thousand defunct satellites that were no longer operational, but nevertheless in orbit, often referred to as 'space junk'. The proposed SpaceX Starlink fleets (or 'constellations' as they are called) therefore constitute a massive increase in the number of satellites in the skies above us, and a correspondingly massive increase of electromagnetic radiation reaching the Earth from outer space.

The SpaceX satellite constellations will not be the only ones. During the 2020s other constellations will also be launched, some serving the same purpose of providing global broadband, others focused on servicing the Internet of Things at somewhat lower frequencies (between 1GHz and 4Ghz). Along with SpaceX, the companies involved in providing broadband include One Web (in partnership with Virgin and Qualcomm), Amazon's Kuiper Systems, the Canadian company Telesat, the American company Leosat as well as Chinese, Russian and Indian state-owned companies. They are each launching their own smaller satellite constellations, and these will bring the total number of projected new broadband satellites to around 20,000 (or, with the extra SpaceX satellites, potentially 50,000) every one of them dedicated to irradiating the Earth at similar frequencies using the same phased array technology.[4]

If we add to this the numerous satellite constellations that will be launched to service the Internet of Things, then during the decade of the 2020s we shall witness an enormous increase in the amount of satellites orbiting the Earth. They will form a kind of 'satellite net' that will capture the planet within an electromagnetic mesh, from which few of us will be able to escape. Figure 4.1 gives an impression, though it is far from complete as it only models the first phase of the Starlink constellation. The electromagnetic mesh that the satellite net will create will be an important part of the new global electromagnetic infrastructure, which is referred to as the fifth generation wireless network or 5G. A simple definition of 5G is that it is a significantly 'upgraded' electromagnetic environment of global extent. It amounts to geo-engineering on a scale never before attempted.

The 5G upgrade is sold to the public as enabling greater amounts of data to be transferred at much faster download speeds, promising an enhancement of the quality of video streaming for media and entertainment, and

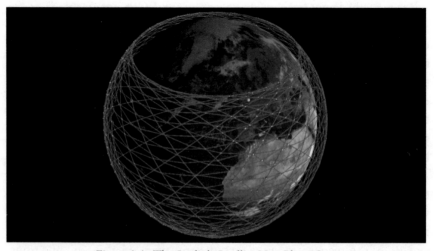

Figure 4.1, The Starlink Satellite Net, Phase One.

providing the means for making both our lives and the planet 'smart'. But to understand it in a more rounded way, we should also consider what effects the new electromagnetic mesh will have on the Earth's living creatures, many of which are attuned to the wider cosmos and to the subtle influences that stream towards the Earth from the planets and stars. While the electromagnetic mesh, or 'electromagnetic ecosystem' as it is called, will enable 'artificial' intelligence systems to function more effectively, we should bear in mind that making the planet 'smart' has two meanings. The intended meaning is the establishment of a global electronic information network, or artificial 'nervous system' for the Earth (as we saw in Chapter 3), at the heart of which is the Internet of Things. The unintended meaning, which lurks beneath this glossy and entirely anthropocentric conception, is of a planet smarting in pain—the pain inflicted on the living Earth, its natural ecosystems and the creatures that belong to them, by the increased levels of radiofrequency radiation that they will have to endure.[5] But the satellite net will have a further environmental impact that has so far been largely overlooked.

The Assault on the Earth's Protective Mantles

When asked how far our planet extends into space, many people might answer that it is as far as the atmosphere extends—just a few miles above the surface of the Earth. In fact beyond the lowest layer of the atmosphere, referred to as the 'troposphere' which embraces the Earth up to a height of about eleven miles, there are important protective sheaths located hundreds of miles above the Earth's surface (Fig. 4.2). These defend the living Earth organism from the incursion of harmful high frequency cosmic rays. The ozone layer in the stratosphere performs a vitally important function in this respect, as does the ionosphere (located in the thermosphere) far above it. Beyond the ionosphere at roughly 435 miles above the Earth is the outermost protective sheath, the magnetosphere, which extends a further 43,000 miles into space on the sun's side. To answer the question of how far our planet extends into space is therefore not so straightforward, for one must surely count the magnetosphere as belonging to the planet, just because it is the planet's outermost defensive sheath.

Some communications satellites orbit as high as 22,200 miles (so-called Geostationary orbit), but the orbital paths of the new satellite constellations will be mainly in the ionosphere, with some further out in lower reaches of the magnetosphere. Since the sole purpose of these satellites is

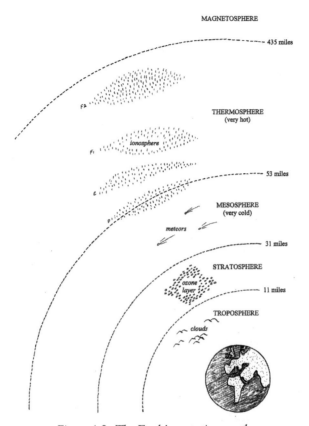

Figure 4.2, The Earth's protective mantles.

to blanket the Earth in electromagnetic radiation, there is a strange irony in their being located within the greater Earth organism's protective mantles. For the purpose of these protective mantles is to ward off harmful electromagnetic radiation from the cosmos. To introduce radiation-emitting satellites into the Earth's protective sheaths seems like an act of deliberate sabotage, but presumably this is not the intention, even though it will be the undoubted effect of the new satellite net.

We must also presume that it is not the intention of the satellite companies to destroy the Earth's protective mantles. Nevertheless, all the satellites have to be taken to their appointed orbital height by rockets, and rocket emissions have a destructive effect on the ozone layer. Furthermore, they contribute to global warming. Given the quantity of planned new satellites, the amount of rocket launches is going to significantly increase in forthcoming years, and with this increase will come an increase in rocket emissions.

Rockets emit several substances that can contribute to climate change and ozone destruction, most importantly black carbon (often called 'black soot'), alumina particles and a highly reactive form of chlorine (called chlorine monoxide). According to a 2010 study, if there were 250 rocket launches globally per year, the black carbon from this number of repeated rocket launches would form a permanent layer in the stratosphere at the northerly latitudes of the launch sites, inducing changes in atmospheric circulation that would result in a warming effect in southern latitudes, especially over the South Pole. This warming effect could be as much as three degrees in the Antarctic during summertime, and could lead to a one degree overall increase in average Antarctic temperature. As a consequence, there would be a 5% decrease in sea ice and a corresponding rise in sea levels.[6] At the same time, it is well known that chlorine monoxide destroys ozone and, when it is mixed with alumina particles, the ozone-destroying reactions are considerably amplified.[7] When ozone is destroyed, more ultra-violet rays penetrate the Earth's atmosphere, with serious consequences for plants, animals and humans.

It is anticipated that by 2025 the number of rocket launches in the USA alone will reach 200—almost twice the number of launches in 2018, and by 2030 the number of launches globally could reach 400, well above the number modelled in the 2010 study.[8] Such a dramatic rise in the number of rocket launches is therefore likely to have a grave impact on the protective ozone layer in the stratosphere above us, as well as on the Earth's atmospheric circulation. We must expect that this will exacerbate climate change and the accompanying rise in sea levels. Given the current global climate emergency, it seems reckless in the extreme to be pressing ahead with a huge increase in the number of satellites in order to establish an electronic ecosystem at such potentially devastating cost to our natural ecosystem.

The Terrestrial 5G Network

As well as the satellite network, 5G will also require hundreds of thousands of new 'small cell' miniature base stations (with multiple miniature antennas) to transmit and receive signals in urban centres throughout the UK, and literally millions of new base stations in cities throughout the rest of the world.[9] These small cell base stations are much less obtrusive than the masts we currently see beside our motorways and on top of buildings. They are discreetly attached to the side of shops and offices or secured to lampposts. Because the terrestrial infrastructure of

small cells will be concentrated in urban environments, one of the purposes of the satellite constellations is to guarantee that rural areas, lakes,
mountains, forests, oceans and wildernesses, where there are neither
buildings nor lampposts, will all be incorporated into the new electronic infrastructure. The aim of 5G, as we have seen, is total coverage
(see Chapter Three, p.58).

At present, mobile phones, smartphones, tablets, Wi Fi and so on all
operate at under 3 GHz in what is called the 'microwave' region of the
electromagnetic spectrum. If you could see and measure their wavelengths, you would find that they are many centimetres (or inches) long.
A smartphone operating at 800 MHz, for example, sends and receives signals with wavelengths of 37.5 centimetres (just under 15 inches). Operating at 1.9 GHz, the wavelengths are 16 centimetres (just over 6 inches).
Wi Fi uses the 2.4 GHz frequency band with 12 centimetre wavelengths
(just under 5 inches). The introduction of 5G will entail the use of much
higher frequencies than these, especially in urban centres utilizing small
cell base stations. These will initially be just below 30 GHz.[10] Above
30 GHz, wavelengths are measured in *millimetres* rather than in centimetres. The millimetre waveband (from 30 GHz to 300 GHz) is referred
to as Extremely High Frequency, and its wavelengths are between 10
millimetres and 1 millimetre in length. The rule is: the higher the frequency at which the wave oscillates, the shorter the wavelength. In the
UK, 5G will initially use the 26 GHz frequency band, with wavelengths
of 1.15 centimetres (11.5 millimetres), in conformity with the Euro-
pean 5G standard, but much higher frequencies will be deployed in the
future, well within the millimetre wave spectrum.[11] Up to the present
time, Extremely High Frequency electromagnetic radiation has not been
widely propagated, and its introduction marks a significant step change
in the kind of electromagnetic energy that will become present in the
natural environment (Fig. 4.3).

The reason why millimetre waves are to be used for 5G is that much
larger bands of spectrum are available in the Extremely High Frequencies than at lower frequencies. This means that there can be much broader
'bandwidth'. Broader bandwidth means that larger quantities of data can
be transferred and the speed of transfer of the data can be a great deal
faster. One of the effects of this is that it reduces what is called 'latency',
or time-lag, in the system so, for example, it improves the quality of video
streaming and enables self-driving cars to respond with lightning speed to
unforeseen circumstances. Greater quantities of data-transfer and reduction

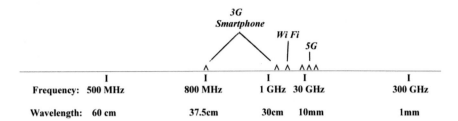

Figure 4.3, Frequencies and wavelengths of smartphone, Wi Fi and 5G.

in latency also allow for a greater seamlessness between our experience of computer-generated virtual content and our perceptions of objects in the real world, as is required in Augmented Reality applications. Greater seamlessness means that we more effortlessly inhabit the natural and the electronic worlds simultaneously, as if they were a single reality.

One of the technical problems of using frequencies in the millimetre region of the spectrum is that, because the waves carrying the data are so tiny, being only millimetres long, they are less able to pass through physical barriers, like walls and trees, than are the longer waves of lower frequencies. This is why it is necessary to have so many more new small cell base stations. The industry calls it 'densification'. Densification means that the small cells are spaced at approximately 100 metres apart in cities because beyond this distance their signal strength weakens and the signals are less able to penetrate buildings, and connect with the devices inside.

Because the wavelengths are so much smaller, the antennas transmitting and receiving them can also be much smaller than those of current phone masts and electronic devices. A single 5G small cell transmitter/receiver will have a large number of tiny antennas, grouped together in one unit. They will enable what is called 'massive MIMO'—or multiple-input/multiple-output, which requires hundreds or thousands of antennas in order to function. According to a 2017 design study, an array of several thousand such antennas measures only four square inches, so will easily fit into a small base station on a lamppost, while the smartphone in your pocket could have as many as 128 antennas.[12]

Both 5G satellites and 5G land-based masts will use a system called the 'phased array'. In the phased array, groups of antennas are co-ordinated to radiate pulses in a specific direction and in a specified time sequence. This allows a concentrated beam of radio waves to be exactly aimed at designated targets, to enable signals to be sent or received with minimal interference. Because the beams are concentrated in this way, this adds to their power, which means they are able more easily to penetrate physical obstacles. But it also means that any living creature that gets in the way of such a concentrated beam will be subjected to a sharp dose of extremely high frequency radiant electricity.

Insects in the Front Line

Studies that have been conducted on the effects of electromagnetic radiation on insects indicate that they are particularly sensitive to radiofrequency fields. For example, in the presence of mobile phones, smartphones, DECT phones or WiFi routers, the motor function of ants is seriously affected and they stagger around as if drunk. In one experiment, when an ants' nest was exposed to a mobile phone the ants were observed to immediately begin to vacate the nest, taking their larvae with them.[13] The ability of fruit flies to grow and reproduce has been shown to be seriously compromised by cell phone radiation. Exposure to a cellphone for six minutes a day for five consecutive days caused the number of eggs laid to be reduced by between 50% and 60%.[14] Other experiments have shown that radiofrequency radiation disrupts the circadian rhythms of cockroaches. And it can completely disorientate bees.[15] Bees are particularly sensitive to radiofrequency electromagnetic fields, reacting to mobile phones placed in the vicinity of a hive by preparing to swarm.[16] These few examples could be multiplied many times over, but are perhaps sufficient to alert us to the likelihood that any further intensification of electromagnetic radiation, especially employing higher frequencies on a global scale, is likely to have an impact not only on these insects, but on others too.

Several studies have shown that, because of their small body-size, insects are especially vulnerable to the millimetre waves of the higher frequencies to be utilized by 5G. The reason is that as the wavelengths decrease in size and begin to approximate the size of the insect, the absorption of the electromagnetic energy increases. For example, a study published in 2011 demonstrated that when termites 12 mm long were exposed to electromagnetic frequencies of 28.24 GHz, at 1.3 Watts power density, they became uncomfortably hot, sending out distress signals. The distress signals drew other termites into the beam, which resulted in all of them dying, huddled together.[17] As small cells will be radiating frequencies very close to this, but at even higher power densities of between 2 and 5 Watts, we may anticipate that not only termites but other insects of roughly the same size will suffer the same effects.

Because insects are incapable of internally regulating their own temperature, they are more susceptible to the heating effects of millimetre wave

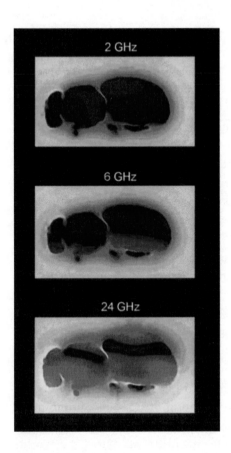

Figure 4.4, Illustration of the absorption of Radio Frequency electromagnetic radiation in the Honeybee. At frequencies up to 6 GHz (top and middle), the wavelength is relatively large compared to the insect's size. But at 24 GHz, (bottom) the wavelength is closer to the insect's size and the radiation penetrates further, causing a pronounced heating effect.

frequencies. A study published in 2018 demonstrated that certain insects absorb more radiofrequency power at and above 6 GHz, and as the frequencies increase the absorption rate goes up.[18] Figure 4.4 shows very vividly what happens to the honeybee when exposed to higher and higher frequencies. In this experiment, the field strength was no more than what many people have in their sitting rooms if they have a router or cordless phone: just under 0.3 Microwatts/cm squared. The colours indicate the Specific Absorption Rate, which measures the heating effect in Watts per Kilogram.

The heating effects of exposure to millimetre waves are likely, at the very least, to lead to changes in the behaviour of the insects so exposed, but the researchers predicted that certain insects would undergo physiological and morphological changes too. As we have seen, exposure to millimetre waves can prove fatal to termites. In recent years, there has been greater awareness of both the vital role that insects play in natural ecosystems, and at the same time the degree to which the number of insects has recently fallen.

In April 2019, a research paper was published detailing the catastrophic collapse of insect populations all over the world. According to the paper, between 2009 and 2019, 41% of insect species declined. Many are heading towards extinction: one third are now regarded as endangered.[19] If anyone were looking for a way of deliberately hastening their decline, it would seem that rolling out 5G with its millimetre wave technology on a global scale could hardly be bettered.

In June 2017, a conference was held in the Netherlands on the topic of 'smart farming', one of the great promises of 5G.[20] Smart farming involves what has come to be known as 'precision agriculture', in which the farmer's day-to-day decision-making draws on vast quantities of data collected through sensors placed in fields, or on air-borne unmanned drones and land-based robots. At the conference, there was discussion on how to respond to the worrying decline of bees. No one mentioned that bees are highly electro-sensitive, a fact which has been known for more than 40 years.[21] The connection between the collapse of bee colonies and exposure to radiofrequency radiation has been repeatedly argued by researchers, but at the smart farming conference a new, 'smart' way forward was presented as the perfect solution to the problem: a new pollinator drone called 'APIS'. The acronym stands for Autonomous Pollination and Imaging System. It is a fully autonomous 'micro air vehicle' designed for greenhouses—one of several currently being developed in different research establishments across the world, including Harvard University.[22] The technical advances that have been made in indoor navigation, miniaturization and precise vision-based control underpin the viability of the design. If our bees are to be killed off by the new electronic ecosystem, never mind! The electronic ecosystem enables them to be replaced with robot bees (Fig. 4.5).

In this one example, the deeper purpose of the electronic ecosystem is laid bare. It will enable intelligent machines, or machine-organism hybrids, to usurp natural organisms. Be assured that the robot bees will become ever more 'bee-like', as their design gradually improves. No doubt they will be deemed to be far more efficient than old-fashioned biological bees. We must wake up to the fact that the technological revolution that we are currently living through goes beyond the extension of our control over nature: it is aiming at the *replacement* of nature with a fully technologized planet. If so many people today were not so enamoured with the flood of seductive gadgets and robotic devices that promise to entertain and empower us, it would be tempting to resort to conspiracy theory to explain what is

Figure 4.5, Robot bee, developed at the Wyss Institute, Harvard University.

happening: a shadowy elite, a hidden agenda. But no, it seems that both nature and essential human values are being undermined by widespread collective enthusiasm for greater and greater technologization of the conditions of life. After all, who doesn't want progress? It is as if something diabolical has got into our souls and cast a spell over us.

Humans Next

I have focused on insects because, owing to their body-size, they are in the front line when it comes to 5G's millimetre waves. We have seen in Chapter Three that there have been a number of studies on the effects of radiofrequency electromagnetic radiation on wildlife, which point to many creatures having an acute sensitivity to electromagnetic fields, and being adversely affected by them.[23] While the biological effects of millimetre wave frequencies have received less recent attention from researchers than sub-30 GHz frequencies, during the 1960s through to the 1990s a large number of studies were conducted on the effects of millimetre wave exposure in the former Soviet Union.[24] Andrei Pakhomov's 1997 review of this research concluded that the biological effects were by no means simply thermal. Organisms as humble as algae, yeast and bacteria, as well as higher plants are sensitive to millimetre waves, which can have the effect both of inhibiting and also stimulating growth depending on the exact frequency, power of the signal and exposure time. With animals, including human beings, it is the surface areas of skin and eyes that are most vulnerable to millimetre waves. Exposure of the skin can lead to knock-on effects such as heart arrhythmia, which was induced in both frogs and rats from exposure of the skin to millimetre waves in areas remote from the heart.[25] Other negative effects include infertility, compromised immune system and cataracts.[26] All of the foregoing effects on animals are likely to apply to human beings—but the decisive experiment is the global rollout of 5G itself—an experiment in which we shall all be obliged to participate.

Much of the research into the biological effects of millimetre wave frequencies does not take into account the beam-forming technology that 5G will use. As well as its ability to concentrate power in focused beams, phased array technology has a further complicating factor. Either side of the main beam, the time intervals between the pulses are different from the time intervals between those of the main beam, but they may overlap each other in such a way as to produce extremely rapid changes in the electromagnetic field. This can have a particularly detrimental effect on living organisms, because instead of the radiation decaying when it is absorbed into living tissue, it can be re-radiated within the body. The moving charges streaming into the body effectively become antennas that re-radiate the electromagnetic field and send it deeper into the organism. These re-radiated waves are known as 'Brillouin precursors', named after the French physicist Leon Brillouin, who first described them in 1914. In 2002, a distinguished American researcher who specialized in Brillouin precursors warned that they can have a highly damaging impact on cells within the body, by inducing a change in electrostatic potential across cell membranes.[27]

This warning echoes that of a Ukrainian research team which, in the year 2000, reviewed the large body of former Soviet Union studies on the biological effects of millimetre wave radiation conducted in previous decades. Commenting on the use of phased array technology to beam millimetre wave electromagnetic radiation from satellites into the Earth's biosphere, they stated that long-term, continuous exposure to such radiation could lead to changes in the genetic apparatus of living cells, and could even result in alteration of behaviour:

> Negative consequences of this may be changes in cell structures and physiological processes, genetic changes, and alteration of psychophysiological conditions and behavior (development of conditioned reflexes).[28]

This warning, given 20 years before the setting up of Starlink and the other satellite constellations, has gone completely unheeded by the space companies and the governmental and intergovernmental agencies that are supposed to regulate them. Is it either wise or ethical to expose the natural environment and all living creatures, including ourselves, to such risks? When we have been warned so explicitly of the potential health consequences of exposure to millimetre wave electromagnetic radiation, using phased array systems, what grounds can there be for assuming that it does not entail any adverse health consequences?

The Un-reassuring Assurances of Government and Industry

The Government body charged with protecting public health in England, Public Health England, advises that there is no convincing evidence that radio frequency radiation (which radio, television, mobile phones, smartphones and 5G all use) has any adverse health effects on either adults or children. This advice is based on the recommendations of a supposedly independent body called AGNIR (Advisory Group on Non-Ionising Radiation), whose 2012 report on the safety of radio frequency radiation is the main source for UK Government policy. The report states that there is a lack of 'convincing evidence' for any adverse health effects.[29] It thereby gives a blank cheque to the telecommunications industry to move on into the higher frequencies, without any heed for the consequences.

In a forensic analysis of the report, the environmental health researcher, Sarah Starkey, makes it clear that only a wilful disregard of the available scientific evidence could explain its internal contradictions and apparent incompetence.[30] Starkey reveals that, far from being independent, AGNIR has a high proportion of members with blatant conflicts of interests, and their report distorts or simply leaves out of account evidence that should have compelled them to reach the opposite conclusion to the one they arrived at. And yet, as the basis of current UK Government policy, it allows the Government to roll out 5G without so much as even a nod towards the need for any prior health and safety assessment.[31] Health and safety simply do not feature in Government thinking, despite a veritable mountain of literally thousands of research papers demonstrating adverse health effects, which continues to grow at the rate of roughly 350 per year, on average practically one every day.[32]

From this abundance of research, Physicians for Safe Technology, a group of sober physicians and health professionals, have gathered the 'convincing evidence' for causal links between exposure to electromagnetic radiation and the development of brain tumours and cancer, neurodegeneration and reproductive abnormalities, etc. that AGNIR was unable to find. They cite the plentiful research that demonstrates the negative effects of EMR on

sperm and ovaries, the liver and kidneys, the immune and endocrine system, the heart, melatonin production, DNA, protein synthesis, the blood
brain barrier, and nerve cell viability and function. They also draw attention
to the emergence of electrosensitivity in the population, with its typical
symptoms of insomnia, headaches, fatigue and impairment of concentration with near exposure to wireless devices, smart meters and cell towers.
For anyone who wishes to inform themselves of the scientific research that
Government and industry prefer to ignore, the Physicians for Safe Technology
website is one of the best places to begin.[33]

One of the reasons for ignoring the scientific research in the hell-for-
leather dash to create the 5G electronic ecosystem is the conviction in
Government circles that, unless we introduce it immediately, we will be
'left behind' and our economic growth and competitiveness will be put at
risk. There is simply no time to consider the possible health consequences.
The National Infrastructure Commission, whose 2016 report, *Connected
Future,* paved the way for the Government's rollout of 5G, pushed this
panicky vision of the UK falling behind other nations and urged the
Government to ensure that the new digital infrastructure is fully in place
by 2025.[34] The NIC report repeatedly points out that the rewards of the
'connected future' are to be measured in billions of pounds worth of
revenue. The mind-boggling amounts involved are well exemplified in an
estimate made by Ovum in 2018, that the global media industry alone
stands to gain $1.3 trillion from 5G by 2025, not least because 5G will
'unlock the potential of Augmented Reality (AR) and Virtual Reality
(VR)'.[35] The irony that the 'connected' future of AR and VR is one that
disconnects us more and more from the real world is entirely missed due,
presumably, to the blinding effect of the profits which stand to be made.

The sums involved are sufficient to explain why the telecoms industry
has for the last 25 years done its utmost to ensure that research into the
health effects of wireless technologies produce negative or inconclusive
results. Since 1993, the industry has financed a large number of studies, saving governments a great deal of expense and at the same time preserving the
convenient illusion that the jury is still out on whether exposure to radio
frequency radiation causes harm. In 2018, *The Guardian* published an article
citing research, which showed that while 67% of independently-funded
studies found a biological effect of exposure to Radio Frequency radiation, only 28% of industry-funded studies did. That means industry-funded
studies are almost two and a half times less likely than independent studies
to find health effects.[36] The authors of the *Guardian* article explain that the

telecoms industry doesn't need to win the scientific argument about safety, but simply keep the argument running indefinitely by producing studies with results that either fail to verify, or even better contradict, the research that does find adverse health effects. One of the most notorious is the mammoth, industry-funded *Interphone Study*, which managed to conclude that holding a mobile phone to the head actually *protects* the user from brain tumours! This study, which is full of contradictions and suffers from grievous design flaws, is often quoted as the most authoritative to date, while it has in fact been thoroughly discredited.[37] Nevertheless, the impression is maintained that because there is no scientific consensus, there are not sufficient grounds for action to be taken. Needless to say, this suits Government just as much as it suits industry.

The Path to Total Immersion

Beyond the health effects there is another level altogether of the multiple assault that the rollout of 5G actually entails. To gain a perspective on this, we should remember that it was not so long ago that the Earth's electromagnetic field was undisturbed by human-generated electromagnetic frequencies. Before the 1880s, there were only two main causes of electromagnetism, both of them natural: the lightning of thunderstorms, which also set in motion the very weak, low frequency resonances known as Schumann Resonances, and sunlight. Lightning and sunlight produce effects in specific, and very limited, parts of the electromagnetic spectrum. The very idea that such a thing as 'electromagnetism' and an 'electromagnetic spectrum' existed was not even entertained before the nineteenth century. And, from the point of view of the pre-electrical age, the truth of the situation was that they indeed did not exist as a factor of experience. Beyond lightning and sunlight, the energies of the electromagnetic spectrum did not impact on human life, for they were entirely dormant (Fig. 4.6).

In that pre-electrical world, both lightning and sunlight were regarded with a certain degree of awe, as natural phenomena expressive of powers greater than anything human beings could muster. In antiquity both were associated with gods—lightning with violent storm gods invariably with Underworld associations, like Seth, Baal and Zeus; and sunlight with sublime solar deities like Ra, Shamash and Apollo. In the later Judaeo-Christian era the widespread sense that these phenomena had a spiritual source persisted, with lightning regarded as expressive of the divine wrath, and the light as the garment of the cosmic Logos. We touch here a deeply felt relationship to nature that has been largely eroded in the centuries since the

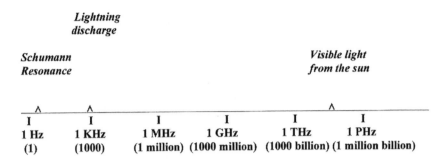

Figure 4.6 Natural background electromagnetic radiation, showing frequencies in cycles per second

Scientific Revolution. In the course of the eighteenth and nineteenth centuries, both lightning and light were stripped of their spiritual numinosity, thereby clearing the way for an entirely materialistic explanation of light, and an entirely technological approach to electricity.

In the early days, the frequencies utilized were at the lower end of the electromagnetic spectrum. In the 1890s, the power lines that delivered the new mains electricity to factories and houses were standardized at either 50 or 60 Hz (or cycles per second). When public radio broadcasts began in the 1920s, they were mostly in longwave frequencies under 500 KHz (thousands of cycles per second). As the century wore on, the frequencies used by new and improved technologies became higher and higher. In the 1930s and '40s, medium and shortwave frequencies (between 500 KHz and 1700 KHz) were utilized, while in the 1950s the Very High Frequencies (VHF) of 30—300 MHz (or millions of cycles per second) were employed for both radio and TV broadcasting. During World War II, a method was discovered for generating Super High Frequencies (3 GHz—30 GHz) of thousands of millions of cycles per second, which became the basis for radar. The advent of mobile phones, smartphones and Wi Fi, brought into widespread use the somewhat lower Ultra High Frequency (UHF) part of the spectrum (300 MHz—3 GHz) for signal transmission. Today, we are poised at the threshold of the new era of combining Super High Frequency (3 GHz—30 GHz) with Extremely High Frequency (30 GHz—300 GHz) to create the global 'electronic ecosystem' (Fig. 4.7). It is important to understand that a great deal of power will be concentrated in the highly focused beams of phased array systems. The environment we live in will not only be fully saturated with an invisible fog of radiation, but it will be shot through with sharp, high-energy, laser-like beams from phased array base stations and 5G devices.[38]

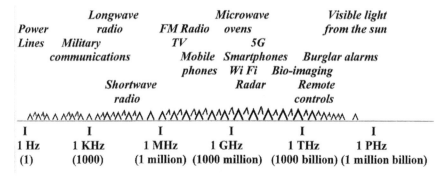

Figure 4.7, Human induced electromagnetic radiation, showing frequencies in cycles per second.

In this brief historical sketch, we see higher and higher frequencies forming the basis of each new technological innovation. As each one of the new technologies was introduced, human beings became a little more disassociated from the natural world. Consider how this happened. From the 1890s onwards, the supply of mains electricity to homes, schools, hospitals and factories caused a revolution in living standards, liberating humanity from subservience to nature's cycles of day and night, summer and winter, by giving access to a new source of light, warmth and power. Then, in the 1920s, radio enabled people to communicate over vast distances, and brought the voices of kings and politicians, singers and poets into our living rooms, even though they were not physically present. In the 1950s, television intensified the experience of an absent yet present world, conveyed by the moving image. As we saw in Chapter Two, one of the effects of television is to draw viewers out of themselves and away from awareness of their immediate surroundings into the fascinating world of images on the screen. With the advent of the smartphone, the trend towards addictiveness was greatly strengthened, partly because the screen became a portable interface with the Internet, and partly because of the deliberately exploitative policies of Facebook, Google and others to hook people into an addictive relationship to their devices.[39] Smartphone addiction both dislocates users from their own inner centre of freedom, and at the same time disconnects them from the natural environment.

5G will further accentuate this tendency of people to lose themselves in thraldom to electronic technologies, and will weaken even more their relationship to nature, for it promises to make advanced immersive Virtual Reality accessible to all. While VR headsets have been commercially available for some time now, VR is still in its infancy. As we have seen in previous chapters, the next development in VR technology will be to make it seem ever more physically real, through for example supplementing the headset with a 'haptic suit', which enables the wearer to experience 'virtually' sensations of touch—pressure, warmth, hardness, softness, moisture and dryness. A report commissioned by Intel in 2018 made the following prediction:

> 5G will start to realize its full transformational potential from 2022 onwards, when we will start to see a significant impact on traditional media usage, mass-scale adoption of AR and VR, and the emergence of new cases such as 3D holographics, haptic suits, and advanced interactive entertainment. Immersive and new media applications will reach an unprecedented scale by 2028, generating in excess of $67bn annually—this is equivalent to the value of the entire mobile media market (video, music, games) last year [2017].[40]

The opportunities to make billions of dollars through 'total immersion' Virtual Reality will no doubt lead to an increasing competition between the electronically generated and the natural world for our sense of where we feel most at home. Just because of the money to be made from it, telecommunications and entertainment companies will do everything they can to encourage the migration of human beings to the virtual world.

The use of Augmented Reality, made possible through headsets, smart glasses, and/or contact lenses, that overlay virtual content onto the experience of the physical world, will add to the competition and to the confusion, as the virtual is increasingly integrated within the real world. We may expect that increasing numbers of people will come to regard the virtual world as having as great a claim on their attention, their emotions and thoughts, as the natural world. One of the major temptations of the future will be for human beings to give their loyalty to that which not only undermines their relatedness to nature but also, through its assault on the imagination, has a corrosive effect on the inner life of the soul. The temptation will only be exacerbated by a huge increase in the use of 3D holographics that will give virtual entities the ability to incarnate electronically in the physical environment. This is what the new electronic ecosystem and the saturation of the world with high frequency millimetre waves will facilitate. The waves themselves are only part of the issue: the technologies that ride on the backs of the waves, impacting our inner life, should also be of utmost concern to us.

The Formation of the Global Electronic Brain

But if 5G promises to radically alter the experiential world we inhabit in these ways, there is something further that we must understand if we are to grasp what is really being prepared for the future. We have seen that, since the 1890s, as more sophisticated electronic technologies have become absorbed into modern culture, so human beings have become increasingly disconnected from the natural world. At the same time, a network of electronic 'intelligence'—global in extent—has gradually emerged. At first it was under close human supervision, but it has steadily grown more autonomous. Consider the difference between radio broadcasting and the Internet: the former is under tight human control and serves a very specific purpose, whereas the latter has established itself as a constantly available electronic infrastructure, with open access and with undefined scope and reach. Over recent decades, intelligence-endowed machines have, through this electronic infrastructure, become increasingly co-ordinated with each other, so they can operate without need of human supervision. The efforts now underway to establish a 5G electronic ecosystem are the necessary precondition for perfecting this autonomous global Artificial Intelligence network, which feeds on the very fast transfer of large amounts of information. Thereby, a global electronic 'brain' comes into existence, innocuously called the 'Internet of Things', and it becomes the foundation of much of our lives.

The Internet of Things, through linking more and more things to the Internet, will also enable them to become 'smart', with the ability to function independently of human beings. On smart motorways your car will drive itself while you, wearing your VR headset and haptic vest, play interactive computer games in the back seat; and in your smart house your fridge will autonomously order more eggs, milk and cheese for you via a wireless connection with a supplier. When we eventually wake up to the new reality that has been created for us, we shall find that the Internet of Things is itself the precursor to what has been called the 'Internet of Thinking'.[41] In the Internet of Thinking, human beings discover that the conditions of life on our planet have become such that we all have to live in relationship to a global electronic intelligence, which will be active everywhere in our environment. We shall be obliged to interact with it in order to accomplish the simplest of tasks. But what actions will we then be able to perform that are truly free? In the current drive to establish a global electronic intelligence, or Global Brain, it is not hard to see the preconditions of electronically supercharged totalitarian states (or a World Government), with unprecedented control over the minutiae of individuals' lives. To step out of line by enacting a truly free initiative may be to risk economic or social exclusion, as is already the case in China. Whatever apparently good things 5G may promise us, what it will put in place will be a lot more than just an improved telecommunications system. It will also put in place the infrastructure of electronic totalitarianism, otherwise known as the 'system of systems'.[42]

A Curtain Drawn Against the Light

As the atmosphere in which we live is increasingly permeated by radio waves, microwaves and millimetre waves, it may seem that the gods of the Underworld have taken hold of humanity in an ever-tightening grip, drawing us towards the false lights—the illusory lights of the hell-beings and hungry ghosts that the *Tibetan Book of the Dead* long ago warned against.[43] The electromagnetic energies that we have summoned, and which promised to give us new powers, now appear to be in danger of overpowering us, carrying us down into an Underworld realm of hellish entertainment and distraction, of illusion and disconnection from the reality that really matters —the reality of nature and of the spiritual order that infuses nature, the reality of the spirit within ourselves, and the reality of fellow creatures with whom we share our world, living in soil and sky and walking the Earth beside us.

We must ask: does the Earth *need* an electronic ecosystem? Is the planet going to benefit in any way from being irradiated with millimetre waves? Is there actually any *need* at all for 5G? Can we even remotely conceive that 5G is the answer to any of the pressing ecological, social and spiritual problems that face us today? We stand at a dreadful threshold, and yet surrender to despair cannot be the right response. What can we do?

First of all we can protest! There are campaigns against 5G that we can join, there are petitions to sign, letters to write, legal actions to support, and the imposition of moratoriums on the rollout of 5G to encourage. But as well as protest there is something further that needs to be done, and that is to bring spiritually informed understanding to the deeper significance of the global electronic brain whose emergence 5G will hasten. To this end, we need to develop a clear perception of the *moral* quality of electricity, the better to recognize the kind of spiritual entity or entities that it serves. This will empower us to break the spell that electricity and electronic technologies have cast over us, and it will enable us to form a more appropriate relationship to them. One of Rudolf Steiner's most helpful insights into electricity was his observation that it is light in a fallen, degraded state— light that has fallen beneath nature into the sub-natural realm—and that is why we must actively guard against an ever increasing dependence on it, for it threatens to drag us down.[44]

This points to a third thing we can do, which is really the foundation of everything else. It is to rebuild our relationship to the light, which in its selfless benevolence and purity greets us every morning, and which, unlike the false and illusory electronic lights that would lead us into the Underworld, beckons us in a quite different direction, towards our essential humanity. Through a deepened meditative relationship to the light, practised through the hours of the day and the seasons of the year, we can nurture a relationship to the inner light that is the source of all that is creative and good in the world. This inner light the Christian tradition knows as the cosmic Logos. As the curtain of electrosmog is drawn across our world, we are presented with a sacred task that, come what may, we attend to all that the light has to give, for therein lies the divine Saving Power.

Chapter Five

BRINGING LIGHT TO THE WORLD: OUR DEEPEST HUMAN VOCATION

Has the Digital Revolution Gone Too Far?

Many people are now questioning where the Digital Revolution is taking us and, more importantly, how we should respond to it. Like the French Revolution, the Digital Revolution was welcomed at first. To many, the transition from analogue to digital technologies that began in the 1970s—for recording sound, photography, communications, data storage and so on—seemed like a quality improvement. Digital technologies belonged to the new computer age, and enabled far greater accuracy and control to be brought to bear on our dealings with the world. But there is a growing sense of apprehension today about the extent to which the Digital Revolution and its wireless networks is altering the very fabric of our lives, with new technologies seeking to bring human beings and machines into ever closer relationship, along with the prospect of the world we inhabit becoming an increasingly hybrid 'cyber-physical' world.

The current rollout of the fifth generation of wireless communication networks, or 5G, has concentrated minds, and aroused unprecedented levels of anxiety about the direction the Digital Revolution is taking. It can seem reminiscent of that moment in the French Revolution when, as the guillotine was first rolled out, the initial euphoria subsided and no one could any longer feel safe. 5G will bring about a massive intensification of the electromagnetic pollution that has accompanied the growth of wireless communications. It will endow Artificial Intelligence systems with even greater power and autonomy, affecting every aspect of our lives. Its extremely rapid rollout, without any prior scrutiny of its potential health effects or environmental impact, is symptomatic of the Digital Revolution having acquired, like the French Revolution before it, a momentum of its own, beyond the constraint of any rational or moral consideration. Where is it taking us? Towards what end? What goal? And in the service of which genuine human needs?

This chapter will explore how we might work towards a spiritual response to the ever more pervasive technologization of the planet, and of our lives. Whatever else we do, whether through protest, political action or simply through taking measures to shield ourselves from intrusive electromagnetic fields, we also need to find ways of strengthening ourselves inwardly, so that we can hold our ground and meet with our full humanity the very powerful forces that threaten to undermine essential human values. These values cannot be understood in isolation from our place in nature and the greater spiritual order to which we belong. The tendency of the Digital Revolution is to dislocate us from these values, and from the dimension of the sacred, both within ourselves and within nature. How, then, can we meet the existential threat posed by extreme technologization, and recover the sacred ground that we need to stand on? How can we work towards a truly human future that, rather than creating yet more pollution and toxicity, brings blessing to the natural world in which we live?

Electromagnetism and Light

Our current situation needs to be seen in context. Both the saturation of the atmosphere with electromagnetic radiation and the development of Artificial Intelligence systems are relatively recent phenomena. Wireless transmission only began towards the end of the nineteenth century. As we saw in Chapter Four, prior to this, the only phenomena of electromagnetism that people were aware of were thunderstorms and sunlight. But neither were regarded as electrical until the eighteenth and the nineteenth centuries respectively, when first lightning and then light were interpreted as electrical phenomena. We are inclined to forget that it was not until the late nineteenth century that the 'electromagnetic spectrum' was discovered: before that, no one suspected that it existed. *Light was the actuality* in this pre-radiofrequency world. It totally filled the atmosphere, and radiant electricity was completely absent (Fig.5.1).

But if light was the actuality, then we must also understand that from time immemorial, this light emanating from the sun and flooding our world each day was experienced as bearing within it a spiritual power. If we go back to ancient Egyptian times, we find abundant evidence of a profound sensitivity to the intrinsically spiritual nature of light. Numerous sacred hymns declare that the light emanates from the life-bestowing sun-god Ra. The omnipresence of light signified that the world was immersed within the divine.[1] We meet a similar awareness in the sacred literature of ancient Israel, where we read how light is the garment that God wraps around himself.[2] This perception of light as the medium through which the divine manifests in the sense-perceptible world was readily taken up in the Christian era. For Dionysius the Areopagite and the mainstream

Christian tradition, light was understood to be an image of the divine goodness, which is revealed in and through it: 'And what of the sun's rays?' asks Dionysius. He answers:

> Light comes from the Good, and light is an image of this archetypal Good. Thus the Good is also praised by the name 'Light', just as an archetype is revealed in its image.[3]

Beyond ancient Egypt, Israel and the Christian tradition, many of the world's cultures and religions attest to the primordial human experience of light as manifesting both a profound spiritual and moral quality, and as mediating the divine presence. This sacred status of light was devastatingly challenged in the 1860s, when the idea of the electromagnetic field was introduced into scientific circles. According to James Clerk Maxwell, who proposed the first comprehensive theory of the existence of an electromagnetic field, light was just one of many different frequencies of radiant electricity. It should be regarded as nothing more than a phenomenon of electromagnetism: it is a disturbance within the greater electromagnetic field, of which it occupies only a tiny portion, and its manifestation is entirely in accordance with electromagnetic laws.[4] Maxwell's theoretical

Figure 5.1, Diagram of light dominating the atmosphere (author's diagram).

formulations were soon experimentally verified by Heinrich Hertz, who declared in 1889, in starkest contrast to Dionysius and so many of the world's religious traditions, that 'light of every kind is an electrical phenomenon'.[5]

From this time on, radiant electricity gradually began to fill the atmosphere as more and more frequencies in the electromagnetic spectrum, each one oscillating at different rates per second, were artificially propagated and utilized for communications. As we saw in Chapter Four, this began with initial experiments in wireless transmission in the late nineteenth century and the first long-wave public radio broadcasts in the 1920s, evolving into FM radio broadcasting and TV in the 1950s, the first compact handheld mobile phones in the 1980s, smartphones in the 2000s and the creation of the 'cyber-physical' Internet of Things with the rollout of 5G in the 2020s (Fig. 5.2). As each new technology was deployed, higher and higher frequencies oscillating at higher and higher rates with shorter and shorter wavelengths, were used so—broadly speaking—we see a movement (from left to right in Fig. 5.2) from low frequencies to high, from long wavelengths to short as we move through the twentieth, and into the twenty-first, centuries. Meanwhile, natural sunlight is reduced to a relatively insignificant narrow band of frequencies in the spectrum of electromagnetic, i.e. essentially subnatural, energies.

In the utilization of the electromagnetic spectrum, we also see a movement from initial sound-broadcasting to the transmission of visual content with the invention of television. The illuminated screen of television introduced human beings to an electronically mediated Otherworld that

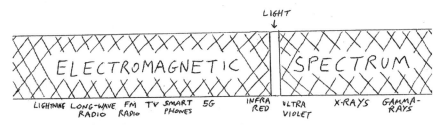

Figure 5.2, Diagram of electromagnetism dominating the atmosphere (author's diagram).

could be regarded as both real and unreal at the same time. When desktop computers acquired a similar screen interface in the 1980s, this gave the user the ability to engage much more directly with machine intelligence. It presented to the user a window into the inner world of the computer, and the electric light that glowed from this window invited the human being in. The electric light was a simulation of natural sunlight, but it exercised a powerful attraction over the human soul because light, especially when it shines through another medium, has an irresistible allure for us. For this reason, the illuminated screen was one of the most psychologically powerful innovations in computer design.

In the desktop computer, and subsequently the laptop, tablet and smartphone, the screen became an entry point into a parallel universe, where human beings would have a growing amount of experiences: communicating with friends, finding things out, conducting business, buying and selling things, and immersion in the fantasy worlds of computer games. Human thoughts, feelings, desires, and fantasies would increasingly be lived out in the arena of machine intelligence. In Figure 5.3, the artificially illumined screen hangs in the sky, with clouds in the background, and the electric glow that emanates from it has usurped the role of sunlight. It is an electronic imposter of the sun. The picture depicts the replacement of the natural light of the sun by the electrically generated light of the computer screen, which now commands the allegiance of the human soul, and casts a spell over human consciousness.

Intelligence and Artificial Intelligence

But what casts the spell is not just the light, it is the peculiarly powerful machine intelligence that it makes available to us, and which seems to become more and more indispensible to our lives. Machine intelligence has the ability to engage us, and to draw us into all that it can do. It is significant that the first electro-mechanical computer was invented at the same time as the early experiments in generating electromagnetic waves and wireless transmission.[6] But just as it is important to understand how light was captured by electricity, so we must also understand how intelligence was captured by machines.

In the Western philosophical tradition, intelligence has long been understood as the distinctively human ability to gain insight into the essence of things. According to both Plato and Aristotle, intelligence (in Greek, *nous*) is a divine endowment that makes human beings active participants in the cosmic spiritual order. Through the gift of intelligence we are able to

Figure 5.3, The lure of the screen.

penetrate the outer appearance of phenomena and grasp their inner spiritual causes. It is, furthermore, a faculty within us which is independent of the physical body, granting us the experience of our own intrinsically spiritual nature.[7] This understanding was transmitted into mainstream Christian philosophy and theology by St Augustine, for whom *intelligentia* is seated in the heart and directed towards what is eternal.[8]

By contrast the modern use of the word intelligence has become almost synonymous with computational ability, a view first advocated in the seventeenth century by Thomas Hobbes. For Hobbes, the activity of thinking is nothing more than making calculations.[9] It was during Hobbes' lifetime that the first mechanical calculators were invented, and he was probably aware of the fact that his definition of intelligence was applicable equally to humans and machines. Defined in terms of calculative ability, intelligence loses its distinctively human attribute: it becomes in the end something merely mechanical.

The assumption that thinking is essentially no different from computing—analysing data, and then making calculations based on this analysis—underlies the graph in Figure 5.4, published in Ray Kurzweil's, *The Singularity is Near* (2005)—a book full of unnerving predictions about the increasing role of Artificial Intelligence in our lives. The graph shows the growth curve

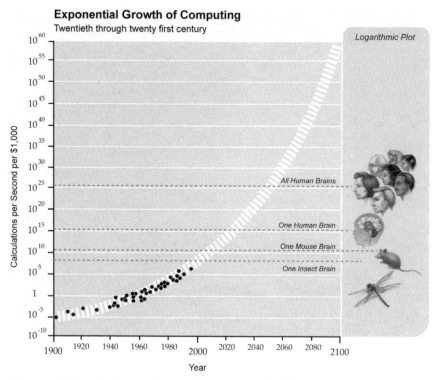

Figure 5.4, Growth of computing according to Kurzweil, The Singularity is Near (2005)

of machine intelligence since 1900, during the days of Hollerith's electro-mechanical computers, through the first electronic computers of the 1940s and 1950s, the personal computers of the 1980s and the early smartphones of the 2000s. During this period both computer memory and processing speeds swiftly increased and could be incorporated in devices commercially available on the mass-market, so the price of machine intelligence rapidly came down. This meant that the amount of 'calculations per second' that could be purchased for $1000 rose exponentially. Kurzweil predicted that calculations per second would continue to rise to the point at which computers equalled and then exceeded human intelligence.[10]

In the graph, machine intelligence is correlated with the intelligence of insects, mice and human beings on a qualitatively indistinguishable continuum. What distinguishes the intelligence of these different creatures is the number of calculations per second each can make. Just as light was absorbed into the electromagnetic spectrum, and defined in terms of a specific number of oscillations per second, so human intelligence merely functions at a certain level of calculations per second. According to the graph, this is a staggering number: several quadrillion (a number with fifteen zeros after it)! Kurzweil predicted that there would be computers capable of such speeds by the year 2020.[11] Where the graph is questionable, however, is not so much in the accuracy of its predictions but in its assumption about the meaning of intelligence. Never mind about the cost or the dates, to measure intelligence in terms of calculations per second has nothing to do with our conscious experience of thinking. Most people, given only one second, would probably fail to make just one calculation, let alone quadrillions! The graph assumes that intelligence can be correlated with electronic or electrochemical activity, but this is very different from our actual *experience* of thinking. From a phenomenological point of view, it is complete nonsense to define intelligence in this way. Nevertheless, this computer model of intelligence and of thinking has become paramount today. As we saw in Chapter Two, p.42, the mainstream view is now that the brain is nothing more than a biological computer, and all human thinking is basically a calculative activity.

This view provides the rationale for the conversion of electrochemical processes in the brain into digital signals, all the better to work more closely with machine intelligence. In Chapter One, p.19 and 23, we noted that headsets that capture our thoughts and convert them into digital signals have been commercially available for some time. Through such technologies, humans gain the ability to interact with, and control, machines by the power of thought alone.[12] As this technology becomes more prevalent, we can only assume that human intelligence will become increasingly enmeshed with Artificial Intelligence. So just as light was purloined by the electromagnetic theory, so we see human thinking hijacked by the reductionist view of human intelligence. Treated merely as an electrochemical process in the brain on the same spectrum as machine intelligence, and conceived as nothing more than 'calculations per second', the path is laid for the atrophy of the deeper spiritual capacities of genuine human intelligence.

How, then, can we reclaim for human intelligence a role that is independent of Artificial Intelligence, and based on an activity that is genuinely free and not simply subservient to the computer-dominated world? With the creeping pervasiveness of the Internet of Things, computational intelligence will be embedded in more and more objects with which we will interact on a daily basis. Therefore it is essential that we take steps to build up the truly human potential of thinking. As we shall see, these steps are closely related to the recognition of the spiritual nature of light.

Recovering the Relationship Between Light and Thought

The relationship between electricity and Artificial Intelligence is one of mutual interdependence. Artificial Intelligence cannot function without electricity. There can be no Artificial Intelligence without electricity, because—as we know—as soon as the power supply goes off or runs out, our computer or smartphone collapses into total inertness. Furthermore, our mobile devices, insofar as they communicate with other devices, receive and emit electromagnetic radiation. Likewise, the embedded sensors, transmitters and actuators crucial to the Internet of Things, and the new 'cyber–physical systems' that 5G will enable, all function by receiving and transmitting radiant electricity. But just as Artificial Intelligence depends upon electricity as its medium, so at the same time electricity finds its fulfilment in Artificial Intelligence. Electricity rises to its highest level when it is digitized in binary code, for then it acquires intelligence, albeit only computational intelligence. Electricity and Artificial Intelligence should thus be regarded as two aspects of a single phenomenon. Figure 5.5 represents this relationship diagrammatically.

This relationship of electricity and Artificial Intelligence has, however, arisen as a kind of mimicking of the relationship of light and thought. Figure 5.5 is in fact adapted from a diagram originally drawn by Rudolf Steiner in 1920 when talking about the relationship of light and thought. In Steiner's diagram, the place of Artificial Intelligence is rightfully taken by thought and that of electricity by light (Fig. 5.6).[13]

When he drew this diagram, Rudolf Steiner's explanation was as follows:

We have the light in us. Only it does not appear to us as light because we live within it, and because while we use the light, it *becomes thought* within us... You take up the light in yourself which otherwise appears outside you. You differentiate it in yourself. You work in it. This is precisely your thinking: it is a working in light... Light and thought go together. They are identical, but seen from different sides.[14]

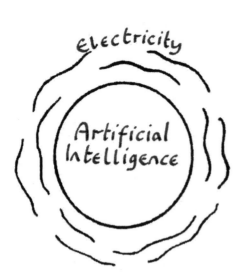

Figure 5.5, Electricity and Artificial Intelligence (author's diagram).

Figure 5.6, Rudolf Steiner's diagram of light and thought.

The idea that thought and light are intimately connected goes back a long way. Perhaps not surprisingly, we find it in Plato, who saw that they are really one and the same entity manifesting outwardly as light, and inwardly as thought or human intelligence (*nous*). For Plato, light and thought both emanate from the same source, which he identified as the Idea of Good. The latter, he says, is.

...the cause of all that is right and good in everything, for it produces in the visible realm light and the source of light [i.e. the sun], and in the intelligible realm it is itself the authentic source of truth and intelligence (*nous*).[15]

This connection of light with the Idea of Good, which not only Plato but also Dionysius and the mainstream Christian tradition recognized, may seem obscure to us today, but each morning we can (if we allow ourselves) feel the sunlit world to be illumining us with the power of goodness. Goodness streams through our bedroom window in the morning sunlight. And this same power of goodness can also be experienced inwardly as giving us the light of waking consciousness, with our ability to think, to know, and to understand.

The intimate relationship between thought and light to which Steiner draws our attention was regarded as quite obvious by other ancient thinkers as well as Plato, for example Aristotle and Plotinus.[16] It was also understood in the Middle Ages. It figures prominently, for instance, in the writings of Thomas Aquinas, for whom 'sense-perceptible light is a certain image of intelligible light'.[17] In ancient and medieval times, thought itself was inwardly experienced as illuminating or shedding light on the world.

After Rudolf Steiner drew this diagram, he added more underneath it. The complete diagram is shown in Figure 5.7.

At the top, the microcosm of the human mind is shown as a small circle, which contains our thoughts. Steiner explains that, seen with spiritual perception, these thoughts are radiating light. At the bottom, the macrocosm of the world is filled with light. But then Steiner says, seen with spiritual perception, this light which is spread out in the world reveals itself to be permeated with

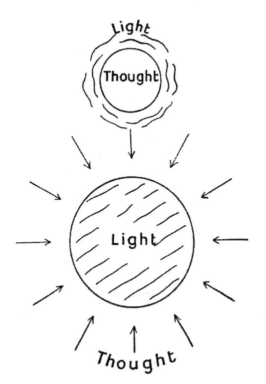

Figure 5.7, Rudolf Steiner's complete diagram of the relationship between light and thought.

thought. Thus *the light we experience in the world around us is permeated with thought.* If we were to ask what is the thought-content that the light holds, philosophers in ancient and medieval times would answer: the light holds the archetypal forms of all creatures. In other words, the inner organising principle of each creature—the spiritual archetype that makes it what it is—is *intrinsically luminous.* One of the great scholars of medieval thought, Etienne Gilson, summarized the traditional Christian metaphysics of light as follows:

All created beings are lights... and their very essence consists in being so many reflections of the divine light. Made up of that multiple of tiny lamps that things are, creation is only an illumination intended to show God.[18]

This view is entirely consonant with that of Rudolf Steiner who, in a lecture given ten years earlier in 1910, made the following statement:

Every substance upon earth is condensed light. There is nothing in material existence in any form whatever which is anything but condensed light... Light cannot be traced back to anything else in our material existence. Wherever you reach out and touch a substance, there you have condensed, compressed light. All matter is, in its essence, light.[19]

So the sense-perceptible universe is a kind of condensation of light in matter. In so far as matter receives the impress of thought, which is what makes each thing what it is, it also receives the impress of light. Figure 5.7 illustrates the fact that this impress is received from the cosmic periphery, which works inwards. But, at the same time, in each living creature the archetype works *from within outwards.* This seeming paradox points us towards how

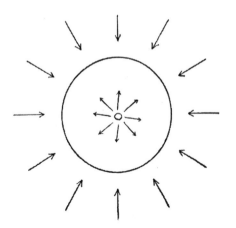

Figure 5.8, From the cosmic periphery inwards, from the spiritual centre outwards (author's diagram).

the forces of life, or the etheric formative forces, act—from the cosmic periphery inwards, and from the spiritual centre outwards (Fig. 5.8). So there is an important overlap between light and the etheric realm: we meet the etheric in light. [20]

Light: a Bridge to the Etheric

One of the things that Steiner says about the nature of light is that although it is present in the world all around us, we do not see it directly, but we see by means of it. It makes things visible, but it is in itself invisible. [21] So when we contemplate light we are contemplating something that, although present in the world, is *essentially a spiritual presence*. It can therefore be regarded as a kind of bridge that leads from the world perceptible to the senses to what is actually extra-sensory. It is *a bridge into the realm of the etheric*.

Light can be our entry point into the etheric because the energies of the etheric, that is to say the formative forces of life, are conveyed through the light; they live in the light. For Steiner, electricity is a force that is inimical to life: it can only animate machines, whereas light is the medium through which the formative forces of life pour into the world.[22] This is something we can all experience, but only through a degree of inner effort, a diligent practice of contemplative observation. The attempt to reach this experience is a first step that we can take to counterbalance the dominance of electromagnetism in the atmosphere, through affirming a greater reality and investing our energies in the exploration of a more profound truth. If we are able to become more conscious of the etheric forces living in the light, this will give us the basis for reclaiming for the light its rightful domain, which is not the realm of electromagnetism but *the realm of life*.

The onus is entirely on us to work towards such a consciousness of the connection between light and the realm of life-forces. It requires that, instead of just taking light for granted, we deepen our relationship to it by, for example, observing the different moods of morning and evening light, and how dawn light differs from the light at dusk; by attending more closely to the constantly changing qualities and interactions of light and shade; by noticing how the varying moisture content of the atmosphere affects the quality of light at different times of day and at different times of year, and how the attributes of light are so very different on a cloudy or sunny day; by focusing on the degree to which light is reflected, transmitted, or absorbed by, for example, leaves and flowers. These are simple but subtle things to observe, but they can sensitize us to the living, spiritual quality of light.

On a sunny day, in particular, we may notice the contrast between how things appear when the source of the light is behind them and when it is in front of them. When backlit, leaves and petals can appear transfigured by the sunlight. It is as if their intrinsic radiance is revealed: then it does not seem so far-fetched to conceive of them as made of condensed light. They can become not just luminous but, as in the case of the tulip in Figure 5.9, actually transparent. At such moments, we may feel we glimpse the presence of spirit in the world of nature, for this can be a numinous experience that arrests our attention, as we contemplate in wonder. And then we may understand something about the allure of the backlit electronic screen: for is it not precisely this numinosity that the backlit screen seeks to replicate? But instead of drawing us into the living etheric world, it draws us into the lifeless electronic world. By immersing ourselves in such phenomena, we may begin to have an intimation of how light bears within itself powerful creative forces.

Coming Home to Thinking

If we consider the lower, macrocosmic part of Steiner's diagram again (Fig. 5.7), it suggests that the more we are able to immerse ourselves in the light, the more we might feel a kind of 'homecoming', for what we meet in the light as sensory experience we also meet within ourselves as an inner experience, namely *thought*. If the light outside us bears within it the cosmic thinking that gives rise to all forms in the world, then it is this same element of thinking that we meet within ourselves, at the centre of our own inner life. Thus human thinking would rightfully occupy a place in the centre of Steiner's macrocosmic diagram, as implicitly belonging to the greater macrocosmic drama (Fig. 5.10). Outwardly, the cosmic logos wraps itself in the garment of light, while inwardly we may come to an experience of the same spiritual power as active in our life of thought.

Figure 5.9, Backlit tulip in Spring (author's photo).

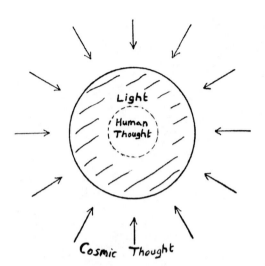

Figure 5.10, Light enclosing cosmic thought; human thought within light (author's diagram).

Like light, the activity of thinking is essentially spiritual, but it is nevertheless present in the sense-perceptible world. So, like light, thinking can also serve as a bridge between the world perceptible to our senses and the spiritual world. But it can only do this if we go beyond the commonly held view that thinking is just a 'calculative' process of logical analysis and reasoning things out. That describes *brain thinking*, but brain thinking is not the essential nature of thinking. Any computer can be programmed to analyze data, but when we truly think we go beyond brain activity and we are active on the *etheric* level. As we have seen, the etheric works from the cosmic periphery inwards and at the same time from the spiritual centre outwards.

Applied to the inner life of thought, this entails, first of all, an act of centring, in which we place ourselves at the inner threshold where thoughts arise. Thereby, we are consciously engaged in the arising of the thoughts—in the act of giving birth to them. The activity of thinking is an opening to what is not yet formed, and giving it form. It requires that we free ourselves of our concepts and our favourite opinions. In this respect, it involves a process of *unthinking* at one level in order to engage more deeply at another level. True thinking is the opposite of falling back on familiar patterns of thought, and it has little to do with analyzing data, or sifting through information and making calculations. Its prerequisite is an *active receptivity* to what arises from within.

But what we give birth to does not exactly arise from within us, in the sense of 'from our own selfhood'. We cannot really claim it as our own. It comes from beyond our ego. We can have the strong sense that the source of our thinking is not really *in us*. It is more that *we are in it*: we are functioning within a greater mind. That is why Steiner says that when we truly think, the spiritual world 'plays into' our thinking. It is a dialogue in which we are not alone. It is a communing with the spiritual world.[23] Figure 5.11 depicts the paradox that the spiritual world within which we exist plays into our thinking

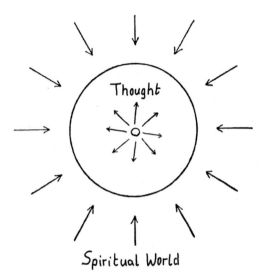

Figure 5.11, How the Spiritual World Plays into Thinking (author's diagram).

from *within* us, and so we may experience our thoughts as arising from a sphere beyond our limited personality. This experience both gives us a taste of thinking as an etheric activity, and it also provides the experiential foundation for rejecting the reductionist view of human intelligence as merely computational. It is thus an essential counterbalance to the current tendency towards ever closer integration of human thinking with Artificial Intelligence systems.

Bringing Light to the World

I have suggested that by immersing ourselves in the living, creative forces borne by the light, we can offer a counterbalance to the saturation of the atmosphere with electromagnetic radiation. Similarly, by deepening our thinking to the point at which we experience it as a living spiritual activity, we can counteract the tendency today of human thinking to become enmeshed with machine intelligence. There is a further vital step that we can also take, as a spiritual response to the influx of extreme technologies into our lives.

One of the most important statements that Steiner makes about thinking as a spiritual activity is that it contains within it 'the power of love in its spiritual form'. When we really engage in thinking—in *living* thinking—it is the power of love that we activate within ourselves.[24] Herein lies a crucial difference between human intelligence and Artificial Intelligence. Human intelligence is intrinsically selfless, which is why it gives us the capacity to enter into the being of another with loving understanding. By contrast, machine thinking is loveless and disconnected from the world. It is locked into the darkness of solipsism, unable to radiate spiritual light.

Both the outer light surrounding us and the light of thinking within us share the same characteristic of intrinsic selflessness. The one illumines all things, great and small, ugly and beautiful, without prejudice; the other enables us through our understanding to illumine the being of another, again without prejudice. This is the power of love in thinking. It directs the light of thinking outwards towards the world.

The activation of this level of thinking within ourselves is our highest calling as human beings. By bringing to the world our loving attentiveness and the warmth of selfless understanding, we are actually bringing life-giving light to the world. And in so doing, we freely bestow a blessing on whatever this light illumines. In one of his meditative verses, Steiner says that the world, without our consciousness of it, would become a frozen waste, empty of life.[25] We could add to that: the more we surrender our consciousness to a world dominated by intelligent machines animated by electricity, the more the world will find only death.

Human beings have something vital, literally vital, to contribute to the world. When we can hold other creatures in the embrace of a loving perception and genuinely selfless understanding, then we are illuminating them; we are bringing light to them. And according to Meister Eckhart, when we illumine other creatures in our understanding, what we are doing is preparing them for their return to God. It is our deepest

Figure 5.12, 'St Francis in the Snow', by Greg Tricker.

human vocation.[26] This is beautifully illustrated in Greg Tricker's painting, *St Francis in the Snow* (Fig. 5.12), in which the saint is portrayed fulfilling this specifically human vocation in a frozen winter landscape.

Each of the three steps I have outlined involves building up our relationship with the light as a spiritual foundation of our response to the technological challenges we face. They will not, of course, stop the rollout of 5G, and after it 6G and 7G, nor will they prevent Artificial Intelligence from becoming increasingly pervasive. They should therefore not be seen as alternatives to political protest or the effort to raise consciousness of the dangers of extreme technologization through reasoned argument based on scientific research. But, by helping us to find the sacred ground on which we can take our stand, they may be thought of as enabling us to place something on the other side of the scales, to counterbalance the negative forces that today assail humanity and menace the living Earth. To take on these forces, we need to fortify ourselves inwardly, and find strength to work towards bringing real blessing to the world.

Notes

Introduction

[1] Lyotard, *The Inhuman: Reflections on Time,* p.2.

[2] Ibid.

[3] Boethius, *The Consolation of Philosophy,* 3.11, poem.

[4] The concept of the 'inner eye' goes back to Plato's *Republic,* 7.4: 518c-d, where he describes how this invisible organ enables us 'to look straight at reality, and at the brightest of all realities, which is what we call the Good'. Through St Augustine, *De Trinitate,* 9-13 (see especially 12: 22-24), Plato's teaching concerning the inner eye entered the mainstream Christian tradition.

[5] Aristotle, *Nicomachean Ethics,* 3.3.17 (1113a17).

[6] Steiner, *The Philosophy of Freedom,* p.140:

> 'We cannot, however, think out the concept of man completely without coming upon the *free spirit* as the purest expression of human nature. Indeed, we are human in the true sense only in so far as we are free.'

See also Aristotle, *Nicomachean Ethics,* 3.3.15-18 (1112b32-1113a9); and Thomas Aquinas, *Summa Theologiae,* 1a2ae: 1.1-4.

[7] 'The whole of this transformation of the human being is summed up by the Fathers in the celebrated formula, "God became man in order that man might become God".' Clément, *The Roots of Christian Mysticism,* p.263.

[8] Dante, *The Divine Comedy: Paradise,* 1.70.

[9] See Chapter Three, p.59 with note 22.

[10] See Chapter Three, notes 21, 23, 26 and 42.

[11] A distinction was commonly made, from the early thirteenth century on, between *Natura naturata* (literally, nature 'natured')—the forms we perceive in the world around us—and *Natura naturans* (literally, nature 'naturing')—the invisible formative forces that unfold into manifestation.

[12] Goethe, 'Problems' (*Probleme,* 1823), translated in Miller, *Goethe: Scientific Studies,* p.44.

[13] As Goethe said: 'The works of nature are like a freshly spoken word of God.' Letter to the Duchess Louise von Saschsen, 28 December, 1789, quoted in Steiner, *Goethe the Scientist,* p.198. Compare with Meister Eckhart who affirmed: 'All things speak God. What my mouth does in speaking and declaring God is likewise done by the essence of a stone.' *Sermons and Treatises,* Volume 1, Sermon 22, p.178.

[14] See, for example, Bonaventure, *The Mind's Road to God,* pp.20-21. This 'theophanic view of nature' is discussed more fully in Naydler, *The Perennial Philosophy and the Recovery of a Theophanic View of Nature.*

[15] The creation of the first synthetic life-form was achieved in 2010 by Craig Venter, based on digitized DNA code. Venter tellingly said at the time: 'It is the first species on the planet to have its parent be a computer.' BBC News, 20 May, 2010.

[16] Rilke, *Letters on Life*, p.61, Letter to Anita Forrer, 14 February, 1920.

Chapter One: Technology and the Soul

[1] Heidegger, *The Question Concerning Technology*, p.28.

[2] Jung, *Memories, Dreams and Reflections*, p.252.

[3] Ibid., p.265.

[4] Ibid., p.252.

[5] Sabini, *The Earth Has A Soul*, p.3.

[6] Jung, *The Structure and Dynamics of the Psyche,* para 802, p.407f.

[7] Ibid,. para 800, p.407.

[8] As described in Slater, 'Cyborgian Drift'.

[9] YouGov, *The Mobile Life Report 2006*. The survey questioned more than 16,500 British adults who use mobile phones.

[10] Ofcom, *Communications Market Report 2016*.

[11] Ibid., pp.30-31

[12] Ibid., p.31.

[13] Turkle, *The Second Self*, p.5.

[14] Ibid., pp.40-41.

[15] Heidegger, *An Introduction to Metaphysics*, p.41f.

[16] Friedman, 'The Age of Interruption'.

[17] *Satipatthana-sutta,* 3. Translated in Rahula, *What the Buddha Taught*, p.111.

[18] IBM System Reference Library, *IBM Operating System/360,* p.64 explains the meaning of 'multitask operation' as follows:

> Each job step is executed as a task... Named load modules are either reused (if they are in storage and reusable) or new copies are fetched. Interruptions are transparent to the user programs. As a result, programs following system conventions that are written for a single-task environment work equally well in multiple-task environments.

[19] See Talbott, *The Future Does Not Compute,* Chapter 1.

[20] Turkle, *Life on the Screen,* was one of the first to explore the psychological permutations of assuming virtual identities (in the mid-1990s). For an overview of the scholarly literature, see Nowak and Fox, 'Avatars and computer-mediated communication', pp.30-53.

[21] Dean, et al., 'Refining Personal and Social Presence in Virtual Meetings'.

[22] Bloom, 'Playing Games With Your Mind'.

[23] Facebook [online blog], 'Facebook is building the future of connection with lifelike avatars', 13 March, 2019. Facebook is by no means the only company investing heavily in this line of research. The Japanese company SoftBank is also developing

the ability to personalize realistic avatars along with various other tech companies. See Nichols, 'Wanted: Realistic avatars for virtual reality meetings', *ZDnet,* 10 August, 2019.

24 The survey was conducted by Google in March 2006 and found that in the United Kingdom the average amount of time that people spent online was roughly 19 hours per week (to be precise, 164 minutes each day). See Johnson, 'Telly Addicts turning into Web Surfers'.

25 Press Association, 'Children spend only half as much time outside'. The survey corroborates the findings of a 2008 study, which estimated that children were spending about half as much time outdoors as children 20 years previously. See Sutherland et al., 'Future novel threats', p.10.

26 Hypergrid Business: *Active Opensim Grids* recorded 314 virtual communities functioning in October 2019.

27 Wikipedia, 'Entropia Universe'.

28 Keegan, 'Screen Grabbers on the Digital Frontier'.

29 The term *mundus imaginalis* was employed by Henry Corbin to refer to an objective 'imaginal' rather than subjective imaginary realm of images. Unlike the latter, the *mundus imaginalis* has objective, supersensible existence, and is accessible to the visionary imagination. See his essay, '*Mundus Imaginalis,* or the Imaginary and the Imaginal', p.18f.

30 Hickey, 'Contact lenses with circuits'.

31 Iyer, et al., 'Inter-Technology Backscatter', ACM, 2016.

32 For an overview, see Royal Society Report, *iHuman,* pp.20-23.

33 See DARPA, 'DARPA and the Brain Initiative', for a summary of the research projects DARPA is engaged in, which includes neural engineering system design, next-generation non-surgical neurotechnology and reliable neural-interface technology, See also Sanchez and Miranda, 'Taking Neurotechnology into New Territory' for a more detailed overview.

34 Memory enhancement, the ability to see in the dark, to access another person's thoughts, and to communicate sensory experiences directly to their brain, are all enhanced cognitive abilities that will be achieved through linking our brains to computers, according to the Royal Society Report, *iHuman,* pp.14-15.

35 See, for example, Kurzweil, *The Age of Spiritual Machines,* pp.277-280; and Brooks, *Robot: The Future of Flesh and Machines,* Chapter 10. See also Humanity Plus [website], 'The Transhumanist Declaration' (2009), which advocates 'human modification and enhancement technologies'.

36 Royal Society Report, *iHuman,* pp.84-85.

37 Heidegger, *The Question Concerning Technology,* p.28.

38 See Jung, *The Symbolic Life,* paras 625-630, and Edinger, *Ego and Archetype,* p.130.

39 Aquinas, *Summa Theologiae,* 1a2ae, 1.1.

Chapter Two: The Quest for the Pearl

[1] For sources of this tradition, see Zaehner, *Hinduism*, p.62. A more detailed discussion (including the Buddhist versions of the teaching) is to be found in Eliade, *The Myth of the Eternal Return*, p.112ff.

[2] Guénon, *The Reign of Quantity*, Chapter 17.

[3] Hesiod, *Works and Days*, 105ff.

[4] Mircea Eliade, op. cit., p.124f.

[5] Naydler, *Temple of the Cosmos,* Chapter 5.

[6] According to Rudolf Steiner, *Kali Yuga* began in 3100 BC and ended in AD 1899. See Steiner, 'The Event of Christ's Appearance in the Etheric World'.

[7] *The Hymn of the Pearl* in Barnstone (ed), *The Other Bible*, pp.308-313. I have greatly simplified the story in the account that follows. For a commentary on *The Hymn of the Pearl*, see Jonas, *The Gnostic Religion*, pp.112-129.

[8] Eliade has frequently commented on this. See, for example, *Myths, Dreams and Mysteries,* Chapter 3 on 'the nostalgia for paradise'; and *The Myth of the Eternal Return,* Chapter 4 on 'the terror of history'.

[9] The prospect of flying saucers taking the faithful to the stars was central to the Heaven's Gate cult, and also had a place in Solar Temple mythology, which envisaged accompanying cataclysmic upheavals on the Earth. See Mayer and Siegler, 'Our Terrestrial Journey is Coming to an End', pp.180-181.

[10] Romanyshyn, *Technology as Symptom and Dream.* See also Cobb, 'Technology's Dream of Abandoning Earth', p.247ff.

[11] *The Times,* 2 October, 1999, p.15. The 1970s precursors of the space hotel were NASA's 'Stanford Torus' and Gerard O'Neill's 'Island One' design concepts, both of which looked forward to an age in which humans would live in outer space for extended periods of time.

[12] 'Nasa to open International Space Station to tourists', BBC News, 7 June, 2019.

[13] Wall, 'Luxury Space Hotel to Launch in 2021', *Space.com,* 5 April, 2018.

[14] Musk, 'Making Humans a Multi-Planetary Species', p.46:

> History is going to bifurcate along two directions. One path is we stay on Earth forever, and then there will be some eventual extinction event. I do not have an immediate doomsday prophecy, but eventually, history suggests, there will be some doomsday event. The alternative is to become a space-bearing civilization and a multi-planetary species, which I hope you agree is the right way to go.

[15] Knapton, 'Human race is doomed'. Enthusiasm for colonizing Mars is shared by another celebrity astrophysicist, Brian Cox. See Cox, 'Why Mars is first for human colonization'.

[16] Garage Staff, 'What does a city of one million people on Mars look like? '

[17] Shagaway, 'Television Recording', p.12.

[18] Postman, *Television and the Teaching of English,* p.30. Postman's source is the US Census Bureau.

[19] Ofcom, *Communications Market Report 2016,* p.5.

[20] Fisher, 'Virtual Environments, Personal Simulation and Telepresence' (1991).

[21] They are used exclusively for the location-based VR company, The Void, which offers 'commercial travel into select parallel dimensions'. The Void website statement continues: 'VOID Travelers can now step beyond their reality into any one of an infinity of possibilities.'

[22] Petrov, '35 Virtual Reality Statistics'.

[23] Pepitone, 'Virtual Reality new tricks'.

[24] Saint Paul, Ephesians, 6:12.

[25] Steiner, *Mystery Knowledge and Mystery Centres,* Lecture 2, 24 November, 1923.

[26] *Vita Adae et Evae* in Charles, *The Apocrypha and Pseudepigraphia of the Old Testament,* p.137. See also the *Koran,* 7.12.

[27] The conversation is recorded in Augustus De Morgan, *Budget of Paradoxes,* pp.249-50.

[28] Monod, BBC interview, quoted in Lewis, *Beyond Chance and Necessity,* p.ix.

[29] Warwick, *The March of the Machines,* p.143.

[30] Walpole, *The Human Machine,* p.5.

[31] Bernal, *The World, the Flesh and the Devil;* Moravec, *Mind Children: The Future of Robot and Human Intelligence.* See also Thompson, *The American Replacement of Nature,* p.122ff.

[32] See, for example, Turing, 'Can Digital Computers Think?' in *The Essential Turing,* p. 483: 'If it is accepted that real brains, as found in animals, and in particular men, are a sort of machine it will follow that our digital computer, suitably programmed, will behave like a brain.' For von Neumann, see *The Computer and the Brain,* pp.38-43.

[33] Pinker, *How the Mind Works,* p.21.

[34] See Lopatto, 'Elon Musk unveils Neuralink's plans'.

[35] Warwick, *The March of the Machines,* p.146; Kurzweil, *The Age of Spiritual Machines,* pp.124-128.

[36] Kurzweil, *The Age of Spiritual Machines,* pp. 128-29.

[37] Roszak, *Where the Wasteland Ends,* Chapter 3; Slater, 'Cyborgian Drift'.

[38] See note 6 above.

[39] See note 6 above.

[40] Jung, 'The Psychology of the Child Archetype' in *The Archetypes and the Collective Unconscious,* §286, p.168.

[41] Discussed in Tradowsky, *Christ and Antichrist,* p.72-73, who points out that Steiner himself believed that by failing the test mankind could sink lower than the level it occupied during *Kali Yuga.*

[42] Not least, the promulgation of Sufi teachings, the Kabbalah, the revival of the Perennial Philosophy and the publication of the Gnostic library discovered at Nag Hammadi. The contemporary world is awash with a wide range of sources of spiritual wisdom.

[43] 'The One Thing You Must Do'. Rumi, *Say I Am You,* p.21 (slightly adapted).

Chapter Three: The Advent of the Wearable Computer

[1] Martin, 'Pebble ships more than 1 million units'.

[2] The Japanese company Seiko (with its subsidiary Epson) produced a series of 'computer watches' in the 1980s, which were able to store a limited amount of information keyed into the watch from an independent keyboard equipped with its own printer. The watches had memo and diary functions, the ability to play simple games and to make calculations. Seiko called the watches 'Wrist Information Systems' but they didn't catch on sufficiently to last into the 1990s. In the 1990s Timex released the Datalink watch, able to synchronise data from a personal computer with which it could communicate wirelessly. It could store numbers, contact information, appointments and so on. But again it didn't last out the decade.

[3] Quoted in Pierce, 'iPhone Killer: the Secret History of the Apple Watch'.

[4] Ibid.

[5] *Statistica*, 'Fitbit device sales—additional information', March, 2019. By 2019, total market sales of Fitbit devices had reached 76 million.

[6] Kothari, 'Glass Enterprise Edition 2', explains that the Glass Enterprise Edition 2 (2019) glasses help workers to:

> …do their jobs more efficiently by providing hands-free access to the information and tools they need to complete their work. Workers use Glass to access checklists, view instructions or send inspection photos or videos.

[7] Quoted in Freeman-Mills, 'Facebook AR Guide'.

[8] Quoted in Crecente, 'Magic Leap'.

[9] Fink, 'The Trillion Dollar 3D Telepresence Gold Mine' discusses the many different systems available, and being developed, for 3D volumetric conferencing using both VR and AR.

[10] Ibid.

[11] Innovega website statement (2019), https://www. emacula.io/#tech.

[12] Ibid.

[13] Quoted in Choi, 'Virtual Reality Contact Lenses'.

[14] HP Labs website statement (2012), https:// hpl.hp.com/research/intelligent_infrastructure/.

[15] At present, the main examples of human subdermal RFID microchipping are in the corporate world, where employees voluntarily agree to have the implants to facilitate access to the workplace, as well as services such as copy machines. See Mearian, 'Office complex implants RFID chips in empoyees' hands'. See also Schwartz, 'The Rise of Microchipping'.

[16] Hern, 'UK homes vulnerable to "staggering" level of surveillance'.

[17] Zuboff, *The Age of Surveillance Capitalism*.

[18] Quoted in John Naughton, 'The Goal is to automate us'.

[19] Cadwalladr and Graham-Harrison, 'How Cambridge Analytica turned Facebook "likes" into a lucrative political tool'.

20 Ofcom, *Update on 5G Spectrum in the UK* (8 February, 2017), p.14:

> Global availability is a primary objective: we see this as essential to provide the environment for a vibrant market in affordable consumer 5G devices.

21 Warnke, 'Bees, Birds and Mankind: Destroying Nature by "Electrosmog"'.

22 For the first estimate, see Philips and Lamburn, 'Natural and Human-activity-generated Electromagnetic Fields on Earth'. For the second, see Bandara and Carpenter, 'Planetary electromagnetic pollution: it is time to assess its impact'. While in non-urban areas it is likely to be considerably less, even were it a billion times less than the levels cited, this would still be respectively a thousand times greater or a billion times greater than natural background levels.

23 See Hardell and Sage, 'Biological Effects from Electromagnetic Field Exposure'. See also Cucurachi et al., 'A review of the ecological effects', who found that 70% of the 113 studies reviewed (from original peer-reviewed publications or from relevant existing reviews) showed a significant effect of EMR on birds, insects and other vertebrates, other organisms and plants. See also Bandara and Weller, 'Biological Effects of Low-intensity Radiofrequency Electromagnetic Radiation'.

24 Matthew Howard, interviewed on *You and Yours*, BBC Radio 4, 25 January, 2012.

25 Ofcom, *Enabling 5G in the UK* (9 March, 2018), pp.3-4, sets out the three frequency 'pipelines' that 5G will use: low-frequency, 700 MHz (due to be auctioned off in 2020); mid-frequency, 3.4 - 3.6 GHz (available since 2019) increasing to 4.2 GHz at some future date; and high-frequency, 26 GHz (currently being tested at the time of writing), with higher bandwidths becoming available in the future. 26 GHz has wavelengths of 11.5 millimeters.

26 See note 23 above. See also Balmori, 'Anthropogenic radiofrequency electromagnetic fields as an emerging threat to wildlife orientation', and Manville 'What We Know, Can Infer, and Don't Yet Know about Impacts from Thermal and Non-thermal Non-ionizing Radiation to Birds and Other Wildlife'. Manville was the senior biologist for the U.S. Fish and Wildlife Service Agency.

27 Johansson, 'Evidence for Effects on the Immune System', *BioInitiative Report*, Section 8, and Gregoriev, 'Evidence for Effects on the Immune System Supplement 2012', *BioInitiative Report,* Section 8. See also Goldsworthy, 'Why Our Urban Trees Are Dying'.

28 There is an overwhelming amount of research that points towards this fact. The research is distributed across a multiplicity of specialist journals. Interested readers may find a useful starting point in the website of *The Environmental Health Trust*: https://ehtrust.org/science/. See also notes 23, 26 and 27 above, and notes 31 and 42 below. See also Chapter Four, note 15.

29 Steiner, *The Agriculture Course,* p.155.

30 Ibid., p.153f.

31 The *Environmental Health Trust* website, https://ehtrust.org/science/research-on-wireless-health-effects/, summarizes the findings of 30 scientific papers published

between 2002 and 2019 demonstrating the neurotoxic effects of exposure to electromagnetic radiation, and eleven papers published between 2008 and 2017 on impaired cognition and memory. The *Electric and Magnetic Fields* website, http://emfs.info/research/abstracts/ alzheimers-abstracts/, provides abstracts of 19 scientific studies specifically on EMFs and Alzheimer's disease, published between 1995 and 2008. See also Davanipour and Sobel, 'Magnetic Field Exposure: Melatonin Production; Alzheimer's Disease; Breast Cancer' *BioInitiative Report*, 2009, Section 9.

[32] Pierce, 'iPhone Killer'.

[33] A helpful overview of Transhumanist thought is given by Bostrom, 'A History of Transhumanist Thought'. See also Harari, *Homo Deus*.

[34] Kurzweil, *The Singularity is Near*, p.9.

[35] Ibid., p.313f.

[36] Ibid., p.29 and pp.361–366.

[37] Three pages of acclaim preface the 2009 edition of the book.

[38] Kurzweil, *The Age of Spiritual Machines*, p.73.

[39] Perera, 'Hawking: Re-engineer humans or risk machine rule'.

[40] Naydler, *In the Shadow of the Machine*, Chapters 12-16.

[41] This is made evident in the writings of twentieth century computer pioneers like Alan Turing and John von Neumann. See, for instance, Turing's seminal essay 'Intelligent Machinery' (1948) in *The Essential Turing*, and von Neumann, *The Computer and the Brain*.

[42] For **trees**, see the *Environmental Health Trust* website, https://ehtrust.org/electromagnetic-fields-impact-tree-plant-growth/, which summarises the findings of twelve research papers published between 2007 and 2017 on the effects of EMR on trees and other plants. For **bees**, the EH Trust website cites 31 articles and reports on the effects of EMR on bees. See also note 21 above, and Wycherley, 'Electromagnetic Pollution Risks to Bees', which gives a recent review of research. For **sparrows and other birds**, see Cucurachi, et al. 'A review of the ecological effects' with note 21 above. See also Mae-Wan Ho, 'Mobile Phones and Vanishing Birds'. For **amphibians**, see Balmori, 'The Incidence of electromagnetic pollution' and 'Mobile Phone Mast Effects'. For **rodents**, see Smith-Roe et al., 'Evaluation Of The Genotoxicity Of Cell Phone Radiofrequency Radiation'. See also the National Toxicology Program fact sheet, 'Cell Phone Radio Frequency Radiation Studies', which summarizes the NTP's ground-breaking Technical Reports published in November 2018. The findings were confirmed by the Ramazzini Institute study in the same year. For discussion see the EH Trust website, https://ehtrust.org/worlds-largest-animal-study-on-cell-tower-radiation-confirms-cancer-link/. For the percentage of the **population suffering from electro-hypersensitivity**, see Bevington, *Electromagnetic Sensitivity and Electromagnetic Hypersensitivity*, p.12 where the estimate is between 3% and 5% of the general population.

[43] Plato, *Republic*, Book 7.4: 518c-d.

Chapter Four: 5G: The Multiple Assault

[1] The orbit of 1,600 of these satellites has since been lowered to 341 miles (550 kms) above the Earth. See Henry, 'FCC OKs lower orbit'. For the frequencies see Brodkin, 'SpaceX plans worldwide satellite Internet'.

[2] Brodkin, 'FCC tells SpaceX'. The figures are for space-to-earth transmissions.

[3] Henry, 'SpaceX submits paperwork'. The satellites would orbit at between 203 and 360 miles above the Earth.

[4] It is a fast–changing situation, but at the beginning of 2020 One Web is aiming for an initial constellation of 650 satellites, eventually increasing to around 2000, Amazon's Kuiper Systems are proposing a constellation of 3,236, Telesat plans to have eventually around 500 satellites and Leosat just over 100 for superfast business connectivity. The Chinese state-owned Chinese Aerospace Science and Technology Corporation is aiming to set up a 150 satellite constellation by 2021, the Russian Space Agency 'Roscosmos' has plans for 640 satellites, while the Indian Space Research Organization is currently boosting its current fleet of communications satellites with some additional high frequency satellites. It is possible that Apple may also enter the satellite communications business too. See Gurman, 'Apple Has Secret Team'.

[5] See Chapter Three, notes 21, 23, 26 and 42.

[6] Ross, et al., 'Potential climate impact of black carbon emitted by rockets'. See also Ross and Toohey, 'The Coming Surge of Rocket Emissions'.

[7] Toohey, 'How do rocket emissions impact ozone and climate?'

[8] Ross and Toohey, 'The Coming Surge of Rocket Emissions'.

[9] According to Small Cell Forum, a telecoms organization driving densification of communications networks worldwide, the installed base of 5G or multimode small cells will reach over 13 million by 2025. See their *Market Status Report*, 20 February, 2018. The UK Government estimates around 40,000 small cells per square mile in urban centres, for which see Department for Culture, Media and Sport and H. M. Treasury, *Next Generation Mobile Technologies* (2017), p.21:

> To give a sense of scale, analysis for the NIC [National Infrastructure Commission] found that as many as 42,000 small cell sites could be needed to deliver the ultra-fast broadband speeds expected of future networks in an area the size of the City of London. By comparison, currently around 40,000 radio access points service the entire UK network.

[10] For the three frequency 'pipelines' that 5G will use in the first phase of its roll-out, see Chapter Three, note 25. The frequencies of the small cell base stations will be 26 GHz, which is very close to the millimetre waveband. Readers should be aware that 26 Ghz is the commonly used shorthand for frequencies between 24.5 GHz and 27.5 GHz. The same caution applies to the figures given in note 11 below: the actual frequency used will be within a band extending either side of the stated figure.

[11] The higher frequencies under discussion are in the region of 32 GHz, 40GHz and 70 GHz. See Rogerson, '5G Frequencies in the UK', See also note 10 above.

[12] Huo, et al., '5G Cellular User Equipment.' The exact number of antennas will depend on the design.

[13] Cammaerts and Johansson, 'Ants can be used as bio-indicators'.

[14] Panagopoulos, et al., 'Effect of GSM 900-MHz Mobile Phone Radiation'. See also Cucurachi et al., 'A review of the ecological effects', who review more recent experiments. The negative effect of exposure to millimetre wave frequencies on the fertility of fruit flies was first observed in the 1970s in the former Soviet Union, as well as morphological abnormalities of pupas and decreased survival of embryos. See Kositsky, et al., 'Influence of High-frequency Electromagnetic Radiation', p. 8 and p. 25.

[15] For cockroaches, see Bartos, et al., 'Weak radiofrequency fields affect the insect circadian clock'. For bees, see Warnke 'Effects of Electric Charges on Honeybees', and Sharma and Kumar, 'Changes in honeybee behaviour'.

[16] Favre, 'Mobile phone-induced honeybee worker piping'.

[17] Tirkel, 'Effects of Millimeter Wave Exposure on Termite Behavior'. Another paper by the same research team demonstrated resonant absorption at 25 GHz, the frequency with a 12mm wavelength. See Tirkel et al., 'Heating Provocation of Termites'.

[18] Thielens, et al., 'Exposure of Insects to Radio-Frequency Electromagnetic Fields', p.9: The insects show a maximum in absorbed radio frequency power at wavelengths that are comparable to their body size... The studied insects that are smaller than 1cm show a peak in absorption at frequencies (above 6 GHz), which are currently not often used for telecommunication, but are planned to be used in the next generation of wireless communication systems.

[19] Sanchez-Bayo and Wyckhuys 'Worldwide Decline of the Entomofauna'.

[20] Smart Farming Conference, Brightlands Campus Greenport Venlo, Netherlands, 29 June, 2017.

[21] Ulrich Warnke wrote a series of research papers on the electro-sensitivity of bees during the 1970s, the best known being 'Effects of Electric Charges on Honeybees', published in 1976. See also notes 15 - 18 above. For a review of recent research, see Wycherley, 'Electromagnetic Pollution Risks to Bees'.

[22] Pluijm and Petrov, 'APIS, the pollinator drone'. Pluijm and Petrov work in the Micro Air Vehicle Lab of Delft University of Technology. Harvard University is another leader in this research. See Spector, 'Tiny Flying Robots'.

[23] See note 5 above. A review of the research into effects of microwave radiation on amphibians, birds, mammals and plants, as well as insects, is given in Firstenberg, *The Invisible Rainbow*, Chapter 16. See also Singer, *An Electronic Silent Spring,* Chapter 3.

[24] Pakhomov, et al., 'Current State and Implications of Research on Biological Effects of Millimeter Waves' gives the number of studies by 1997 on the biological effects of millimetre waves in the former Soviet Union as 463, while in the rest of the world the number was 261, making a total of 624. Most of the research in the former Soviet

Union, however, was focused on possible medical and therapeutic effects of clinical exposure to millimeter waves, rather than the risk to public health of widespread environmental exposure.

25 Ibid.

26 For infertility, see Kositsky, et al., 'Influence of High-frequency Electromagnetic Radiation', p.24. For immune response and cataracts, see Russell, 'A 5G Wireless Future', pp.20-23, who reviews some of the research. See also Ciaula, 'Towards 5G communication systems: Are there health implications?' p.367, who summarizes the health implications as follows:

> MMW increase skin temperature, alter gene expression, promote cellular proliferation and synthesis of proteins linked with oxidative stress, inflammatory and metabolic processes, could generate ocular damages, [and] affect neuro-muscular dynamics.

27 Oughstun, interview on 'Brillouin Precursors', p.10. According to Oughstun, a professor of electrical engineering and mathematics at the University of Vermont:

> A single Brillouin precursor can open small channels through the cell membrane because, as it passes through the membrane, it can induce a significant change in electrostatic potential across that membrane.

28 Kositsky, et al., 'Influence of High-frequency Electromagnetic Radiation', p.18. The team assumed prolonged exposure to low-energy electromagnetic radiation from communication satellites transmitting between the frequencies of 20 GHz and 30 GHz, with a power of 800 watts, at an orbital height of 870 miles (1400 km), considerably higher than the orbits of most of the planned 5G satellite constellations.

29 Report of the Advisory Group on Non-Ionising Radiation, *Health Effects from Radiofrequency Electromagnetic Fields*, p.3:

> No consistently replicable effects have been found from RF field exposure at levels below those that produce detectable heating. In particular, there has been no convincing evidence that RF fields cause genetic damage or increase the likelihood of cells becoming malignant. Studies of animals have employed a wide range of biological models, exposure levels and signal modulations. Taken together, these studies provide no evidence of health effects of RF field exposures below internationally accepted guideline levels. In particular, well-performed large-scale studies have found no evidence that RF fields affect the initiation and development of cancer, and there has been no consistent evidence of effects on the brain, nervous system or the blood-brain barrier, on auditory function, or on fertility and reproduction.

30 Starkey, 'Inaccurate official assessment of radiofrequency safety.'

31 The Department for Culture, Media and Sport and H. M. Treasury, *Next Generation Mobile Technologies* (2017), which sets out the Government's strategy for the rollout of 5G, does not mention health and safety precautions.

32 One of the best sources for this mountain of research is *The BioInitiative Report*, (2012/2019), https://bioinitiative.org/table-of-contents, which helpfully gathers it

into manageable sections, and is regularly updated. According to the Report, between 2007 and 2012, approximately 1800 new studies demonstrated adverse health effects, i.e. on average 350 per year.

[33] *Physicians for Safe Technology,* https://mdsafetech.org/science. Another essential online resource is *The BioInitiative Report,* for which see note 32 above.

[34] National Infrastructure Commission, *Connected Future* (December, 2016), p.11. The authors argue that only by so doing could the UK 'take full advantage of technologies such as artificial intelligence and augmented reality.'

[35] Ovum, *How 5G Will Transform the Business of Media and Entertainment,* p.3. The report was commissioned by Intel.

[36] Hertsgaard and Dowie, 'The inconvenient truth about cancer and mobile phones' (2018). The blatant funding bias was first exposed in 2006 by Slesin, '"Radiation Research" and the Cult of Negative Results'. A good summary of the problem is given in Powerwatch [website], 'Bias and Confounding in EMF Science'.

[37] *The Interphone Study* is devastatingly critiqued in Morgan, et al., *Cellphones and Brain Tumors* (2009), p.8.

[38] Firstenberg, '5G—From Blankets to Bullets' explains:

> At 50 GHz, an array of 1,024 antennas will probably not be that large—tens or hundreds of watts. But… arrays containing such large numbers of antennas will be able to channel energy into highly focused beams, and the *effective* radiated power will be enormous.

So enormous, in fact, that the Senior Expert for Electromagnetic Fields and Health at the Swedish telecommunications company, Ericsson, stated in a presentation given in December 2017 that the size of the exclusion zone (safety zone) around a 5G base station would have be so large that it would make the 5G network roll-out 'a major problem or impossible'. See Törnevik, 'Impact of EMF limits on 5G network roll-out'.

[39] Goddard, 'Facebook exploits human weakness'.

[40] Ovum, *How 5G Will Transform the Business of Media and Entertainment,* p.5.

[41] Williams, 'Welcome to the Internet of Thinking'.

[42] Nokia, *5G—a System of Systems.* For the infrastructure of totalitarianism, see Chapter Three, p.58.

[43] *Tibetan Book of the Dead,* p.43f:

> Do not take pleasure in the soft smoky light of the hell-beings… If you are attracted to it you will fall down into hell, and sink into the muddy swamp of unbearable suffering from which there is never any escape… Do not be attracted to it, do not yearn for it. Feel longing for the luminous, brilliant, white light [of wisdom].

[44] Steiner, *Anthroposophical Leading Thoughts,* p.218.

Chapter Five: Bringing Light to the World

1 Assmann, *Egyptian Solar Religion*, p.81.

2 Psalm 104:

> Yahweh my God, how great you are!
>
> clothed in majesty and glory,
>
> wrapped in a robe of light!

3 Dionysius, *Divine Names*, 4.4, 697c, p.74. This view of light as an image of a spiritual archetype is taken up by Aquinas in his *Commentary on the Gospel of John*, Lecture 2.

4 Maxwell, 'A Dynamical Theory of the Electromagnetic Field' (1864), §97, p.500.

5 Hertz, 'On the Relations Between Light and Electricity', p.313.

6 In the 1880s, when Hertz was conducting his experiments on electromagnetic waves, Herman Hollerith designed and built his 'tabulating machine', the first electro-mechanical computer, which was successfully employed in the American census of 1890. Hollerith's company was later consolidated into IBM. The 1890s saw the first experiments in wireless transmissions by Sir Oliver Lodge and Marconi.

7 Plato, *Timaeus*, 90b-c; Aristotle, *Metaphysics* 10.3.8, and *Nicomachean Ethics*, 10.7.8.

8 Augustine, *Confessions*, 7.17. Later authors, such as Boethius and Aquinas tended to use the word *intellectus* rather than *intelligentia*, but it referred to the same human faculty: the centre of spiritual intelligence.

9 Hobbes, *Leviathan*, I, 5.

10 Kurzweil, *The Singularity is Near*, Chapter 3.

11 In 2019 the fastest computer (a gigantic supercomputer in China) reached the speed of 93 quadrillion operations per second. But it costs considerably more than $1000, so it wouldn't yet feature on this graph.

12 The company Emotiv Inc., for example, which specializes in neurotechnology, offers a range of affordable headsets, and promises to enable the user to 'control machines with the power of your mind'.

13 Rudolf Steiner, 'Thought and Will as Light and Darkness'.

14 Ibid.

15 Plato, *Republic*, Book 6: 517b-c.

16 At the beginning of the *Physics*, Aristotle describes the path of investigation as running from what is directly accessible to our cognition to what is intrinsically intelligible, which he characterizes as being a path from the less light-filled (sense-perceptions) to the more light-filled intelligible forms of things: 'Hence, in advancing to that which is intrinsically more luminous and by its nature accessible to deeper knowledge, we must needs start from what is more immediately within our cognition...' See *Physics*, 1.1: 134a17-21.

This is echoed in Plotinus, *Enneads*, V.5.7: 16-21, p.409, where the intellect (*nous*) 'sees by another light the objects illuminated by the First Principle: so long as the light is within them, it sees; declining towards the lower nature, that upon which the light from above rests, it has less of that vision. Passing over the visible and looking to the medium by which it sees, then it holds the Light and the source of Light.' According to Schroeder, 'Plotinus and Language', p.343, for Plotinus 'the procession of sensible from intelligible reality is not merely *likened* to the procession of light from its source. It *is* such a procession.'

[17] '*Lux autem ista sensibilis, imago quaedam est illius lucis intelligibilis*'. Thomas Aquinas, *Commentary on the Gospel of John*, 8.2, §1142. For Aquinas's theology and metaphysics of light, see Whidden, *Christ the Light*.

[18] Gilson, *History of Christian Philosophy in the Middle Ages*, p.120.

[19] Steiner, 'Free Will and Karma in the Future of Human Evolution' (27 May, 1910), *Manifestations of Karma*, p.188.

[20] Barfield, 'The Light of the World'. See also Rudolf Steiner, *The Light Course*, Lecture 5 (27 December, 1919), p.92.

[21] Steiner, *The Story of My Life*, p.64:

> Light is not really perceived by the senses; colours are perceived by means of light, which manifests itself everywhere in the perception of colours but it is not itself sensibly perceived.

[22] Steiner, *The Agriculture Course*, pp.153-155. Steiner warned that filling the atmosphere with radiant electricity would have detrimental effects on human beings and on all living organisms, because electricity doesn't belong to the realm of life, but tends to undermine it.

[23] Steiner, lecture of 5 January, 1919, quoted in Palmer, *Rudolf Steiner on his Book, 'The Philosophy of Freedom'*, p.21f.

[24] Steiner, *Philosophy of Freedom*, p.119.

[25] Steiner, *The Calendar of the Soul*, 33, p.136:

> 'The world, without my soul's experience of it, would be a frozen waste, empty of life... and itself would find only death.'

[26] Eckhart, *Sermons and Treatises*, vol.2, Sermon 56, pp. 80-81 (translation adapted):

> All creatures enter my understanding that they may be illumined in me. Thereby I prepare all creatures for their return to God.

SOURCES

Sources of the Chapters

The chapters in this book were originally published as independent articles or essays. They have all been substantially revised and updated for publication in the present volume.

The seed of the Introduction and the title of the book was sown in 2009 in a talk given for the Jupiter Trust, Oxford, subsequently published as a booklet: *The Struggle for a Human Future* (Oxford: Abzu Press, 2009).

Chapter One: 'Technology and the Soul'. First published as a booklet by Abzu Press, Oxford in 2008, and subsequently published in *New View*, 49 (2008), pp.7-15. It originated as a talk given at the Temenos Academy in London, on 7 February, 2007.

Chapter Two: 'The Quest for the Pearl'. First published by Abzu Press, Oxford, in January 2000, it originated as a talk given for the Jupiter Trust, Oxford, in October 1999.

Chapter Three: 'The Advent of the Wearable Computer'. First published in *New View*, 65 (2012), pp.12-19; *Self and Society*, 40.3 (2013), pp.17-24. Subsequently published as a booklet by Abzu Press, Oxford, 2013.

Chapter Four: '5G: The Multiple Assault'. First published as '5G: The Final Assault' in *New View*, 90 (2019), pp.33-40.

Chapter Five: 'Bringing Light to the World'. First published in *New View*, 93 (2019), pp.3-11. This originated as a talk given at the Anthroposophical Society Summer Conference, Emerson College, 2019.

Illustration Sources

1.1 Jung's retreat at Bollingen. Photo: Ruth Ammann, Jung Institut, Zurich.

1.2 Sleeping with the iPhone. Rawpixel.com.

1.3 New Yorker Cartoon by Peter Steiner, reproduced by permission of Cartoon Collections.

1.4 Pokemon Go. Photo: Charlie Danger.

1.5 Bionic contact lens. University of Washington.

2.1 The fantasy of abandoning the earth: the astronaut as the new technological shaman. The astronaut Bruce McCandless II, Space Shuttle Challenger mission, 7 February, 1984. Photo courtesy of NASA.

2.2 International Space Station, June 2011. Courtesy of NASA. S134-E-010592.

2.3 Television: inhabiting an inner world that is not our own. *Movie Audience* (1979) by Jeff Wall. Courtesy of the artist.

2.4 Entering virtual space, exiting real space. From Scott S. Fisher, 'Virtual Environments, Personal Simulation and Telepresence'. NASA Ames VIEWlab System Prototype 3, 1988. Photo credit: NASA/S. S. Fisher, W. Sisler, 1988.

2.5 Iblis refuses to bow down before Adam. Early Fifteenth century painting from a ms. of the Persian rendition of Bal'ami, *Annals (Tarikh) of al-Tabari*. Topkapi Palace Museum Library. Wikimedia Commons.

2.6 'The human body is a fascinating and remarkable machine.' From Brenda Walpole, *The Human Machine* (Hove: Wayland, 1991), p.11.

2.7 The archangel Michael struggles with Satan. Watercolour painting by William Blake, *Michael Binding Satan* (1805). Wikimedia Commons.

3.1 Pebble Smart watch. April, 2012. Wikimedia Commons.

3.2 Google Glass face-mounted wearable computer. July 2012.

3.3 Deflected from the real to the virtual cob. GoogleGlass app.

3.4 Enabling an artificially 'intelligent' planet. Publicity image from Advantech's website, 2012.

4.1 The Starlink Radiation Net. Mark Handley, University College, London.

4.2 The Earth's protective sheaths. Author's diagram.

4.3 Frequencies and wavelengths of smartphone, Wi Fi and 5G. Author's diagram.

4.4 The absorption of Radio Frequency electromagnetic radiation in the honeybee. Source: Arno Thielens, et al., 'Exposure of Insects to Radio-Frequency Electromagnetic Fields from 2 to 120 GHz', Nature, 8: 3924 (2018), fig.4.

4.5 Robot bee, Wyss Institute, Harvard University.

4.6 Natural background electromagnetic radiation, showing frequencies in cycles per second. Author's diagram.

4.7 Human induced electromagnetic radiation, showing frequencies in cycles per second. Author's diagram.

5.1 Diagram of light dominating the atmosphere. Author's diagram.

5.2 Diagram of electromagnetism dominating the atmosphere. Author's diagram.

5.3 The lure of the screen. Source unknown.

5.4 Exponential growth of computing, according to Kurzweil, *The Singularity is Near* (2005), p.70. Used by permission of Viking Books, an imprint of Penguin Publishing Group, a division of Penguin Random House LLC.

5.5 Electricity and Artificial Intelligence. Author's diagram.

5.6 Rudolf Steiner's diagram of light and thought. From Rudolf Steiner, *Colour* (London: Rudolf Steiner Publishing Company, 1935).

5.7 Rudolf Steiner's complete diagram of the relationship between light and thought. From Rudolf Steiner, *Colour* (London: Rudolf Steiner Publishing Company, 1935).

5.8 From the cosmic periphery inwards, from the spiritual centre outwards. Author's diagram.

5.9 Backlit tulip in Spring. Author's photo.

5.10 Light within cosmic thought; human thought within light. Author's diagram.

5.11 How the Spiritual World Plays into Thinking. Author's diagram.

5.12 'St Francis in the Snow', by Greg Tricker. With the kind permission of the artist.

BIBLIOGRAPHY

Advisory Group on Non-Ionising Radiation (AGNIR). *Health Effects from Radiofrequency Electromagnetic Fields*. Health Protection Agency, 2012.

Aquinas, Thomas, *Summa Theologiae*. Translated by Thomas Gilby. London: Blackfriars in conjunction with Eyre and Spottiswoode, 1969.

——*Commentary on the Gospel of John*. Albany, NY: Magi Books, 1998.

Aristotle. *Nicomachean Ethics*. Loeb Classical Library. London: Heinemann, 1975.

—— *Metaphysics*. Loeb Classical Library. London: William Heinemann, 1975.

—— *Physics*. Loeb Classical Library. London: William Heinemann, 1934.

Assmann, Jan. *Egyptian Solar Religion in the New Kingdom*. Abingdon: Routledge, 2009.

Augustine. *The Confessions of St Augustine*. Translated by F. J. Sheed. London: Sheed and Ward, 1948.

Balmori, Alfonso. 'The Incidence of electromagnetic pollution on the amphibian decline'. *Toxicological and Environmental Chemistry*, 88.2 (April-June, 2006), pp.287-299.

—— 'Mobile Phone Mast Effects on Common Frog (*Rana* temporaria) Tadpoles'. *Electromagnetic Biology and Medicine*, 29.1-2 (2010), pp.31-35.

——'Anthropogenic radiofrequency electromagnetic fields as an emerging threat to wildlife orientation'. *Science of the Total Environment*, 518-519 (July, 2015), pp.58-60.

Bandara, Priyanka and Steve Weller. 'Biological Effects of Low-intensity Radiofrequency Electromagnetic Radiation—Time for a Paradigm Shift in Regulation of Public Exposure'. *Radiation Protection in Australia* (Journal of the Australasian Radiation Protection Society), 34.2 (November 2017), pp.2-6.

Bandara, Priyanka and David O. Carpenter. 'Planetary electromagnetic pollution: it is time to assess its impact'. *The Lancet*, 2 (December 2018), pp.512-514.

Barfield, Owen. 'The Light of the World' in Supplement to *Anthroposophical Movement*, 31.2 (February, 1954). Reprinted in *New View*, 93 (October-December, 2019), pp.12-20.

Barnstone, Willis (ed). *The Other Bible*. San Francisco: Harper and Row, 1984.

Bartos, Premsyl et al. 'Weak radiofrequency fields affect the insect circadian clock'. *Journal of the Royal Society: Interface*, 16:20190285 (2019). http://dx.doi.org/10.1098/rsif.2019.0285.

Bernal, J. D. *The World, the Flesh and the Devil*. 1929; London: Jonathan Cape, 1970.

Bevington, Michael. *Electromagnetic Sensitivity and Electromagnetic Hypersensitivity: A Summary*. London: Capability Books, 2013.

Bloom, James, 'Playing Games With Your Mind'. *The Guardian*, 21 February, 2008.

Boethius. *The Consolation of Philosophy*. Loeb Classical Library. Cambridge MA: Harvard University Press, 1973.

Bonaventure. *The Mind's Road to God.* Translated by George Boas. Indianapolis: Bobbs-Merrill, 1953.

Bostrom, Nick. 'A History of Transhumanist Thought'. *Journal of Evolution and Technology*, 14. 1 (2005).

Brodkin, Jon. 'SpaceX plans worldwide satellite Internet with low latency, gigabit speed', *Ars Technica*, 17 November, 2016. https://arstechnica.com/information- technology/2016/11/spacex-plans-worldwide-satellite-internet-with-low-latency-gigabit-speed.

—— 'FCC tells SpaceX it can deploy up to 11,943 broadband satellites'. *Ars Technica* 15 November, 2018. https://arstechnica.com/information-technology/2018/11/spacex- gets-fcc-approval-for-7500-more-broadband-satellites.

Brooks, Rodney A. *Robot: The Future of Flesh and Machines*. London: Penguin, 2002.

Cadwalladr, Carole and Emma Graham-Harrison. 'How Cambridge Analytica turned Facebook "likes" into a lucrative political tool'. *The Guardian*, 17 March, 2018.

Cammaerts, Marie-Claire and Olle Johansson. 'Ants can be used as bio-indicators to reveal biological effects of electromagnetic waves from some wireless apparatus'. *Electromagnetic Biology and Medicine*,33.4 (2013).

Charles, R. H. *The Apocrypha and Pseudepigrapha of the Old Testament in English,* vol. 2. Oxford: Oxford University Press, 1913.

Choi, Charles Q. 'Virtual Reality Contact Lenses Could be Available by 2014'. *Scientific American*, 2 February, 2012. https://scientificamerican.com/article/virtual-reality-contact-1.

Ciaula, Agostino Di. 'Towards 5G communication systems: Are there health implications?' *International Journal of Hygiene and Environmental Health*, 221.3 (April 2018), pp.367-375.

Clément, Olivier. *The Roots of Christian Mysticism*. London: New City, 1993.

Cobb, Noel. 'Technology's Dream of Abandoning Earth'. *Temenos* 11 (1990), pp.247-249.

Copeland, Jack, ed. *The Essential Turing*. Oxford: Clarendon Press, 2004.

Copenhaver, Brian P. *Hermetica: The Greek* Corpus Hermeticum *and the Latin* Asclepius *in a New English Translation with Notes and Introduction*. Cambridge: Cambridge University Press, 1972.

Corbin, Henry. '*Mundus Imaginalis,* or the Imaginary and the Imaginal' in Henry Corbin, *Swedenborg and Esoteric Islam*. Translated by Leonard Fox. West Chester, Penn.: Swedenborg Foundation, 1995.

—— *Alone with the Alone: Creative Imagination in the Sufism of 'Ibn Arabi*. Princeton: Princeton University Press, 1997.

Corpus Hermeticum. See Copenhaver.

Cox, Brian. 'Why Mars is first for human colonization and then beyond'. *National Geographic*, 26 March, 2018.

Crecente, Brian. 'Magic Leap: Founder of Secretive Start-Up Unveils Mixed-Reality Goggles'. *Variety Magazine*, 20 December, 2017. https://variety.com/2017/gaming/news/1202870280.

Cucurachi, S. et al. 'A review of the ecological effects of radiofrequency electromagnetic fields (RF-EMF)'. *Environment International*, 51 (January 2013), pp.116-140.

DARPA [website]. 'DARPA and the Brain Initiative'. https://darpa.mil/program/our-research/darpa-and-the-brain-initiative.

Davanipour, Z. and E. Sobel. 'Magnetic Field Exposure: Melatonin Production; Alzheimer's Disease; Breast Cancer'. *BioInitiative Report*, 2009, Section 9. https://bioinitiative.org/table-of-contents.

Dean, Jesse, Mark Apperley and Bill Rogers. 'Refining Personal and Social Presence in Virtual Meetings' (Proceedings of the Fifteenth Australasian User Interface Conference, 2014, Auckland, New Zealand), in Burkhard Wünsche and Stefan Marks, eds., *Conferences in Research and Practice in Information Technology*, vol.150. Sydney: Australian Computer Society, 2014, pp.67-75.

Department for Culture, Media and Sport and H. M. Treasury. *Next Generation Mobile Technologies: A 5G Strategy for the UK*, March, 2017. https://www.gov.uk/government/publications/next-generation-mobile-technologies-a-5g-strategy-for-the-uk.

Dionysius the Areopagite. *Divine Names*. In *Pseudo-Dionysius: The Complete Works*. Translated by Colm Luibheid. New York: Paulist Press, 1987.

Easton, Stewart. *Man and the World in the Light of Anthroposophy*. New York, Anthroposophic Press, 1975.

Eckhart, Meister. *Sermons and Treatises*. Volumes 1-3 . Translated and edited by M. O'C. Walshe. Shaftesbury: Element Books, 1979-1987.

Edinger, Edward F. *Ego and Archetype*. Boston: Shambhala Publications, 1972.

Eliade, Mircea. *The Myth of the Eternal Return*. Princeton: Princeton University Press, 1954.

———— *Myths, Dreams and Mysteries*. London: Collins, 1968.

Facebook [online blog]. 'Facebook is building the future of connection with lifelike avatars',

Facebook.com, 13 March, 2019. https://tech.fb.com/codec-avatars-facebook-reality-labs.

Favre, Daniel. 'Mobile phone-induced honeybee worker piping'. *Apidologie*, 42.3 (2011), pp.270-279.

Fink, Charlie. 'The Trillion Dollar 3D Telepresence Gold Mine'. *Forbes*, 20 November, 2017. https://forbes.com/sites/charliefink/2017.

Firstenberg, Arthur. *The Invisible Rainbow: A History of Electricity and Life*. Santa Fe, New Mexico: AGB Press, 2017.

—— '5G—From Blankets to Bullets'. https://www.cellphonetaskforce.org/5g-from-blankets- to-bullets.

Fisher, Scott S. 'Virtual Environments, Personal Simulation and Telepresence' in S. Helsel and J. Roth, eds. *Virtual Reality: Theory and Practice and Promise*. Westport; London: Meckler, 1991.

Forster, E. M. *The Machine Stops*. London: Penguin, 2011. First published in *The Oxford and Cambridge Review*, November, 1909.

Franz, Marie-Louise von. *Alchemy.* Toronto: Inner City Books, 1980.

Freeman-Mills, Max. 'Facebook AR Guide: An Exploration into Zuck's Augmented Reality Plans'. *Wareable,* 2 September, 2019. https://wareable.com/ar/facebook.

Friedman, Thomas. 'The Age of Interruption'. *New York Times,* 5 July, 2006.

Garage Staff. 'What does a city of one million people on Mars look like?'. *HP: The Garage,* 14 August, 2018. https://garage.ext.hp.com/us/en/innovation/innovation-hp-mars-home-planet-challenge-renderings.

Gerson, Lloyd P. ed. *The Cambridge Companion to Plotinus.* Cambridge: Cambridge University Press, 1996.

Gilson, Etienne. *History of Christian Philosophy in the Middle Ages.* London: Sheed and Ward, 1980.

Goddard, Jacqui. 'Facebook exploits human weakness, admits former boss Sean Parker'. *The Times,* 10 November, 2017.

Goldsworthy, Andrew. 'Why Our Urban Trees Are Dying'. *Bio Electromagnetic Research Initiative.* 2011, https://bemri.org/publications/wildlife-and-plants/plants/355-why-our-urban-trees-are-dying.

Gregoriev, Yuri. 'Evidence for Effects on the Immune System Supplement 2012: Immune System and EMF RF'. https:// bioinitiative.org/table-of-contents.

Guénon, René. *The Reign of Quantity and the Signs of the Times.* London: Luzac and Co, 1953.

Gurman, Mark. 'Apple Has Secret Team Working on Satellites to Beam Data to Devices'. *Bloomberg,* 20 December, 2019. https://www.bloomberg.com/news/articles/2019-12-20/apple-has-top-secret-team-working-on-internet-satellites.

Harari, Yuval Noah. *Homo Deus: A Brief History of Tomorrow.* London: Penguin Random House, 2015.

Hardell, Lennart and Cindy Sage. 'Biological Effects from Electromagnetic Field Exposure and Public Exposure Standards'. *Biomedicine and Pharmacotherapy,* 2.62 (February, 2008), pp.104-109.

Heidegger, Martin. *The Question Concerning Technology.* Translated by W. Lovitt. New York: Harper and Row, 1977.

—— *An Introduction to Metaphysics.* Translated by Ralph Manheim. New Haven and London: Yale University Press, 1959.

Henry, Caleb. 'FCC OKs lower orbit for some Starlink satellites'. *Space News,* 26 April, 2019. https://spacenews.com/fcc-oks-lower-orbit-for-some-starlink-satellites.

——'SpaceX submits paperwork for 30,000 more Starlink satellites'. *Space News,* 15 October, 2019. https://spacenews.com/spacex-submits-paperwork-for-30000-more-starlink-satellites.

Hern, Alex. 'UK homes vulnerable to "staggering" level of surveillance'. *The Guardian,* 1 June, 2018.

Hertsgaard, Mark and Mark Dowie. 'The inconvenient truth about cancer and mobile phones'. *The Guardian,* 14 July, 2018.

Hertz, Heinrich. 'On the Relations Between Light and Electricity'. *Miscellaneous Papers*. London: MacMillan, 1896.

Hesiod. *Works and Days and Theogony*. Translated by Stanley Lombardo. Indianapolis/ Cambridge: Hackett Publishing Company, 1993.

Hickey, Hannah. 'Contact lenses with circuits, lights a possible platform for super-human vision,'. *UW News*, 17 January, 2008. https://www.washington.edu/news/2008/01/17/contact-lenses-with-circuits-lights-a-possible-platform-for-superhuman-vision.

Ho, Mae-Wan. 'Mobile Phones and Vanishing Birds'. *Science in Society,* 34 (2007).

Hobbes, Thomas. *Leviathan* (1651). London: J. M. Dent and Sons, 1973.

Humanity Plus [website]. 'The Transhumanist Declaration' (2009). https://humanityplus.org/philosophy/transhumanist-declaration.

Huo, Yiming et al. '5G Cellular User Equipment: From Theory to Practical Hardware Design'. *arXiv:1704.02540v3* (2017). https://arxiv.org/pdf/1704.02540.pdf.

Hymn of the Pearl in Willis Barnstone, ed. *The Other Bible*. San Francisco: Harper and Row, 1984.

Hypergrid Business [website]. *Active Opensim Grids,* November 2019. https://hypergridbusiness.com/statistics/active-grids.

IBM System Reference Library. *IBM Operating System/360: Concepts and Facilities*. New York: International Business Machine Corporation, 1965.

Iyer, Vikram, et al. 'Inter-technology Backscatter: Towards Internet Connectivity for Implanted Devices'. Association for Computing Machinery, 2016. http://interscatter.cs.washington.edu/files/interscatter.pdf.

Johansson, Olle. 'Evidence for Effects on the Immune System'. *BioInitiative Report*, Section 8, https:// bioinitiative.org/table-of-contents.

Johnson, Bobbie. 'Telly Addicts turning into Web Surfers'. *The Guardian*, 8 March, 2006.

Jonas, Hans. *The Gnostic Religion*. Boston: Beacon Press, 1963.

Jung, C. G.. *Memories, Dreams and Reflections*. Translated by Richard and Clara Winston. London: Fontana Press, 1995.

—— *The Structure and Dynamics of the Psyche*. CW 8. Translated by R. F. C. Hull. London: Routledge and Kegan Paul, 1969.

—— *The Symbolic Life*. CW 18. Translated by R. F. C. Hull. London: Routledge and Kegan Paul, 1977.

——'The Psychology of the Child Archetype' in *The Archetypes and the Collective Unconscious*. CW 9:1. Translated by R. F. C. Hull. London: Routledge, 1980.

Keegan, Victor. 'Screen Grabbers on the Digital Frontier'. *The Guardian Weekly*, 30 November, 2007.

Knapton, Sarah. 'Human race is doomed if we do not colonise the Moon and Mars, says Stephen Hawking'. *The Telegraph,* 20 June, 2017.

Kositsky, Nikolai et al. 'Influence of High-frequency Electromagnetic Radiation at Non-thermal Intensities on the Human Body' (2000). Translated in *No Place To Hide—*

Newsletter of the Cellular Phone Taskforce Inc., Volume 3, Number 1—Supplement, February 2001. https://buergerwelle.de/assets/files/influence_of_high_frequency_electromagnetic_radiation_at_non_thermal_intensities.pdf?cultureKey.

Kothari, Jay. 'Glass Enterprise Edition 2: Faster and More Helpful'. *Google* [web blog], 20 May, 2019. https:// blog.google/products/hardware/glass-enterprise-edition-2.

Kurzweil, Ray. *The Age of Spiritual Machines.* London: Penguin, 2000.

———— *The Singularity is Near.* London: Duckworth, 2005.

Lewis, John, ed. *Beyond Chance and Necessity.* London: Garnstone Press, 1974.

Lopatto, Elizabeth. 'Elon Musk unveils Neuralink's plans for brain-reading "threads" and a robot to insert them'. *The Economist,* 16 July, 2019.

Lyotard, Jean-François. *The Inhuman: Reflections on Time.* Translated by Geoffrey Bennington and Rachel Bowlby. Cambridge: Polity Press, 1993.

Manville, Albert M. 'What We Know, Can Infer, and Don't Yet Know about Impacts from Thermal and Non-thermal Non-ionizing Radiation to Birds and Other Wildlife'. *Wildlife and Habitat Conservation Solutions,* 2014, available from *Environmental Health Trust,* 14 July, 2016. https:// ehtrust.org/science/bees-butterflies-wildlife-research-electromagnetic-fields-environment.

Martin, Brandon. 'Pebble ships more than 1 million units'. *Inferse,* 2 February, 2015. https:// inferse.com/22340.

Maxwell, James Clerk. 'A Dynamical Theory of the Electromagnetic Field' (1864). *The Scientific Papers of James Clerk Maxwell,* Volume 1. Edited by W. D. Nixon. Cambridge: Cambridge University Press, 1890.

Mayer, Jean-François and Elijah Siegler. '"Our Terrestrial Journey is Coming to an End": The Last Voyage of Solar Temple'. *Nova Religio: The Journal of Alternative and Emergent Religions,* Vol. 2, No. 2 (April 1999), pp.172-196.

Mearian, Lucas. 'Office complex implants RFID chips in employees' hands.' *Computer World,* 6 February, 2015. https://computerworld.com/article/2881178/office-complex-implants-rfid-chips-in-employees-hands.

Miller, Douglas. *Goethe: Scientific Studies.* New York: Suhrkamp Publishers, 1988.

Moravec, Hans. *Mind Children: The Future of Robot and Human Intelligence.* Cambridge, Mass: Harvard University Press, 1988.

Morgan, Augustus De. *Budget of Paradoxes.* London: Longmans Green and Co., 1872.

Morgan, L. Lloyd et al. *Cellphones and Brain Tumors: 15 Reasons for Concern* (2009). http://electromagnetichealth.org/pdf/Cellphones%20and%20BT-15%20Reasons-for-Concern-USA1s.pdf.

Musk, Elon. 'Making Humans a Multi-Planetary Species'. *New Space,* 5.2 (June, 2017).

National Infrastructure Commission. *Connected Future* (December, 2016). https://www.gov.uk/government/publications/connected-future.

National Toxicology Program [fact sheet]. 'Cell Phone Radio Frequency Radiation Studies'. https://niehs.nih.gov/health/materials/cell_phone_radiofrequency_radiation_studies_5 08.pdf.

Naydler, Jeremy. *Temple of the Cosmos: The Ancient Egyptian Experience of the Sacred*. Rochester, VT, Inner Traditions International, 1996.

—— *The Perennial Philosophy and the Recovery of a Theophanic View of Nature*. London: Temenos Academy, 2018.

—— *In the Shadow of the Machine: The Prehistory of the Computer and the Evolution of Consciousness*. Forest Row: Temple Lodge, 2018.

Naughton, John. '"The Goal is to automate us": welcome to the age of surveillance capitalism'. *The Guardian*, 20 January, 2019.

Neumann, John von. *The Computer and the Brain*. New Haven: Yale University Press, 1958.

Nichols, Greg. 'Wanted: Realistic avatars for virtual reality meetings'. *ZDnet*, 10 August, 2019. https://zdnet.com/article/wanted-realistic-avatars-for-virtual-reality-meetings.

Nokia Solutions and Networks [White Paper]. *5G—a System of Systems* (2015). http://www.iot.gen.tr/wpcontent/uploads/2016/08/nokia_5g_systems_of_systems_white_paper.pdf.

Nowak, K. and J. Fox. 'Avatars and computer-mediated communication: a review of the definitions, uses, and effects of digital representations'. *Review of Communication Research*, 6 (2018), pp.30-53. https://doi.org/10.12840/ issn.2255-4165.2018.06.01.015.

Ofcom. *Communications Market Report 2016*. https://ofcom.org.uk/research-and-data/multi-sector-research/cmr/cmr16.

—— *Update on 5G Spectrum in the UK* (8 February, 2017). https://www.ofcom.org.uk/__data/assets/pdf_file/0021/97023/5G-update- 08022017.pdf?source=post_page.

—— *Enabling 5G in the UK* (9 March, 2018). https://www.ofcom.org.uk/__data/assets/pdf_file/0022/111883/enabling-5g-uk.pdf.

Oughstun, Kurt. Interview on 'Brillouin Precursors', *Microwave News*, 22, 2 (2002).

Ovum. *How 5G Will Transform the Business of Media and Entertainment*. Informa Telecoms and Media Ltd., October, 2018. https://newsroom.intel.com/wp-content/uploads/sites/11/2018/10/ovum—intel—5g.

Pakhomov, Andrei et al. 'Current State and Implications of Research on Biological Effects of Millimeter Waves: A Review of the Literature'. *McKesson BioServices*, 1997, https://www.rife.org/otherresearch/millimeterwaves.

Palmer, Annie. 'Japanese scientists develop genetically modified "Frankenstein" pigs with organs that can be transplanted into humans'. *The Daily Mail*, 8 March, 2018.

Palmer, Otto. *Rudolf Steiner on his Book, 'The Philosophy of Freedom'*. New York: The Anthroposophic Press, 1975.

Panagopuolos, Dimitris, et al. 'Effect of GSM 900-MHZ Mobile Phone Radiation on the Reproductive Capacity of *Drosophila melanogaster*'. *Electromagnetic Biology and Medicine*, 23.1 (2004), pp.29-43.

Pepitone, Julianne. 'Virtual Reality's new tricks: How it fools your brain into having a "real" experience'. *HP: The Garage,* 13 August, 2019, https://garage.ext.hp.com/us/en/innovation/Virtual-reality-experiences-tricks-the-senses.

Perera, Rick. 'Hawking: Re-engineer humans or risk machine rule'. *PC World,* 4 September, 2001, https:// pcworld.idg.com.au/article/print/39817.

Petrov, Christo. '35 Virtual Reality Statistics That Will Rock the Market in 2019'. *TechJury,* 9 April, 2019. https://techjury.net/stats-about/virtual-reality.

Philips, Alasdair and Graham Lamburn. 'Natural and Human-activity-generated Electromagnetic Fields on Earth', (7 October, 2012). http://bemri.org/publications/natural-fields/427-natural-and-human-activity-generated-electromagnetic-fields-on-earth.

Pierce, David. 'iPhone Killer: the Secret History of the Apple Watch'. *Wired,* April, 2015, https://wired.com/2015/04/the-apple-watch.

Pinker, Steven. *How the Mind Works.* New York: Norton, 1997.

Plato. *Timaeus.* Loeb Classical Library. Cambridge, MA/London: Harvard University Press, 2005.

——*The Republic.* Two volumes. Loeb Classical Library. Cambridge MA/London: Harvard University Press, 1937.

Plotinus. *Enneads.* Translated by Stephen Mackenna. London: Faber and Faber, 1956.

Pluijm, Anthony Van der and Aleksandar Petrov. 'APIS, the pollinator drone'. Delft University of Technology, Micro Air Vehicle Lab. Smart Farming Conference, 29 June 2017, Venlo. https://smartfarmingconference.com/speaker/apis-pollinator-drone-presented-anthony-van-der-pluijm-aleksandar-petrov-delft-university-technology.

Postman, Neil. *Television and the Teaching of English.* New York: Appleton-Century-Crofts, inc., 1961.

Powerwatch [website]. 'Bias and Confounding in EMF Science'. https://powerwatch.org.uk/science/bias.asp.

Press Association. 'Children spend only half as much time outside as their parents did'. *The Guardian,* 27 July, 2016.

Rahula, Walpola. *What the Buddha Taught.* New York: Grove Press, 1974.

Rilke, Rainer Maria. *Letters on Life.* Edited and translated by Ulrich Baer. New York: Random House, 2005.

Romanyshyn, Robert D. *Technology as Symptom and Dream.* London: Routledge, 1989.

Rogerson, James. '5G Frequencies in the UK'. *5G Guides,* 6 June, 2019. https://5g.co.uk/guides/5g-frequencies-in-the-uk-what-you-need-to-know.

Ross, Martin et al. 'Potential climate impact of black carbon emitted by rockets'. *Geophysical Research Letters,* 37, L24810 (2010). https://doi.org/10.1029/2010GL044548.

Ross, Martin and Darin Toohey, 'The Coming Surge of Rocket Emissions', *Earth and Space Science News,* 24 September, 2019. https://eos.org/features/the-coming-surge-of- rocket-emissions.

Roszak, Theodore. *Where the Wasteland Ends.* London: Faber and Faber, 1972.

Royal Society Report. *iHuman: blurring lines between human and machine,* September 2019. https://royalsociety.org/topics-policy/projects/ihuman-perspective/

Rumi, Jelaluddin. *Say I Am You.* Translated by Coleman Barks. Maypop Press, 1994.

Russell, Cindy. 'A 5G Wireless Future'. *The Bulletin* (January/February, 2017), pp.20-23. https://ecfsapi.fcc.gov/file/10308361407065/5%20G%20Wireless%20Future-SCCMA%20Bulletin_FEb%202017_pdf.

Sabini, Meredith, ed. *The Earth Has A Soul: The Nature Writings of C. G. Jung.* Berkeley: North Atlantic Books, 2002.

Saint Paul, Letter to the Ephesians. *The New Testament: New International Version.* London: Hodder and Stoughton, 2011.

Sanchez, Justin and Robbin Miranda. 'Taking Neurotechnology into New Territory', *Defense Media Network,* 14 March, 2019. https://defensemedianetwork.com/stories/taking-neurotechnology-new-territory/4.

Sanchez-Bayo and Wyckhuys. 'Worldwide Decline of the Entomofauna'. *Biological Conservation,* 232 (April 2019). pp.8-27.

Schroeder, Frederick. 'Plotinus and Language' in Lloyd P. Gerson, ed. *The Cambridge Companion to Plotinus.* Cambridge: Cambridge University Press, 1996.

Schwartz, Oscar. 'The Rise of Microchipping: Are We Ready for Technology to Get Under the Skin?'. *The Guardian,* 8 November, 2019.

Shagaway, Robert. 'Television Recording—the origins and earliest surviving live TV broadcast recordings'. *Early Television Museum,* April, 2011. http://earlytelevision.org/tv_recordings_the_origins.

Sharma, V. P. and Kumar, N. K. 'Changes in honeybee behaviour and biology under the influence of cellphone radiations'. *Current Science,* 98.10 (2010), pp.1376-1378.

Singer, Katie. *An Electronic Silent Spring.* Great Barrington, MA: Portal Books, 2014.

Slater, Glen. 'Cyborgian Drift: Resistance is not Futile'. *Spring* 75.1 (2006), pp.171-195.

Slesin, Louis. '"Radiation Research" and the Cult of Negative Results'. *Microwave News,* 26.4 (July, 2006), pp.1-5.

Small Cell Forum. *Market Status Report.* 20 February, 2018. http://www.scf.io/en/documents/050__Small_cells_market_status_report_February_2018.php.

Smith-Roe, Stephanie L. et al. 'Evaluation Of The Genotoxicity Of Cell Phone Radiofrequency Radiation In Male And Female Rats And Mice Following Subchronic Exposure'. *National Toxicology Program,* September 2017. https://www.emfsa.co.za/research-and-studies/ntp-peer-reviewed-paper-on-dna-breaks-induced-by-cell-phone-radiation-published.

Spector, Dina. 'Tiny Flying Robots Are Being Built To Pollinate Crops Instead of Real Bees'. *Business Insider,* 7 July, 2014. https://www.businessinsider.com.au/harvard-robobees-closer-to-pollinating-crops-2014-6.

Starkey, Sarah J. 'Inaccurate official assessment of radiofrequency safety by the Advisory Group on Non-ionising Radiation'. *Review of Environmental Health,* 31:4 (2016), pp.493-503.

Statistica [website]. 'Fitbit device sales—additional information', March, 2019. https://statistica.com/statistics/472591/.

Steiner, Rudolf. 'The Event of Christ's Appearance in the Etheric World' (25 January, 1910), in *The True Nature of the Second Coming*. London: Anthroposophical Publishing Company, 1961.

—— *Mystery Knowledge and Mystery Centres*. London: Rudolf Steiner Press, 1997.

—— *The Influences of Lucifer and Ahriman*. London: Rudolf Steiner Publishing Co., 1954.

—— *Goethe the Scientist*. New York: Anthroposophic Press, 1950.

—— *The Agriculture Course*. Translated by George Adams. Forest Row: Rudolf Steiner Press, 2004.

—— *Anthroposophical Leading Thoughts*. Translated by George and Mary Adams. Forest Row: Rudolf Steiner Press, 1973.

—— 'Thought and Will as Light and Darkness' (5 December, 1920), in *Colour*. Translated by H. Collison. London: Rudolf Steiner Publishing Company, 1935.

—— 'Free Will and Karma in the Future of Human Evolution' (27 May, 1910), in *Manifestations of Karma*. Translated by Heidi Herrmann-Davey. Forest Row: Rudolf Steiner Press, 1995.

—— *The Light Course*. Translated by Raoul Cansino. Great Barrington, MA: Anthroposophic Press, 2001.

—— *The Story of My Life*. Translated by H. Collison. London: Anthroposophical Publishing Company, 1928.

—— *The Philosophy of Freedom*. Translated by Michael Wilson. London: Rudolf Steiner Press, 1964.

—— *The Calendar of the Soul*. Translated by Christopher Bamford. Great Barrington, MA: SteinerBooks, 2003.

Sutherland, W. J. et al. 'Future novel threats and opportunities facing UK biodiversity identified by horizon scanning'. *Journal of Applied Ecology*, March 2008.

Talbott, Stephen. *The Future Does Not Compute*. Sebastopol, Ca: O'Reilly and Associates, Inc., 1995.

Thielens, Arno et al. 'Exposure of Insects to Radio-Frequency Electromagnetic Fields from 2 to 120 GHz'. *Nature*, 8: 3924 (2018). https://doi.org/10.1038/s41598-018-22271-3.

Thompson, William Irwin. *The American Replacement of Nature*. New York: Bantam Doubleday Dell, 1991.

Tibetan Book of the Dead. Translated with commentary by Francesca Fremantle and Chögyam Trungpa. Boston and London: Shambhala, 1987.

Tirkel, A. Z. 'Effects of Millimeter Wave Exposure on Termite Behavior'. *Progress in Electromagnetic Research Symposium Proceedings, Marrakesh, Morocco,* (March 20-23, 2011), pp.1581-1585.

—— 'Heating Provocation of Termites Using Millimeter Waves'. *PIERS Proceedings, Marakesh, Morocco* (March 20-23, 2011), pp.1586-1589.

Toohey, Darin. 'How do rocket emissions impact ozone and climate?' *Atmospheric and Oceanic Studies, University of Colorado* (2011). http://atoc.colorado.edu/~toohey/basics.

Törnevik, Christer. 'Impact of EMF limits on 5G network roll-out'. *ITU Workshop on 5G, EMF and Health,* 5 December, 2017. https://itu.int/en/ITU-T/Workshops-and- Seminars/20171205/Documents/S3_Christer_Tornevik.pdf.

Tradowsky, Peter. *Christ and Antichrist.* London: Temple Lodge, 1998.

Turing, Alan. *The Essential Turing.* Edited by Jack Copeland. Oxford: Clarendon Press, 2004.

Turkle, Sherry. *The Second Self: Computers and the Human Spirit.* Cambridge MA: The MIT Press, 2005.

—— *Life on the Screen: Identity in the Age of the Internet.* New York: Simon and Schuster, 1995.

Vita Adae et Evae in R. H. Charles, *The Apocrypha and Pseudepigrapha of the Old Testament in English,* vol. 2. Oxford: Oxford University Press, 1913.

Void [website]. http:// thevoid.com.

Wall, Mike. 'Luxury Space Hotel to Launch in 2021'. *Space.com,* 5 April, 2018. https:/space.com/40207-space-hotel-launch-2021-aurora-station.html

Walpole, Brenda. *The Human Machine.* Hove: Wayland, 1990.

Warnke, Ulrich. 'Effects of Electric Charges on Honeybees'. *Bee World,* 57.2 (1976), pp.50- 55.

—— 'Bees, Birds and Mankind: Destroying Nature by "Electrosmog".' Competence Initiative for the Protection of Environment, Humanity and Democracy, (2009). https://ecfsapi.fcc.gov/file/7521097894.pdf.

Warwick, Kevin. *The March of the Machines.* London: Century, 1997.

Whidden, David L. *Christ the Light: the Theology of Light and Illumination in Thomas Aquinas.* Augsberg, MN: Fortress Press, 2014.

Wikipedia. 'Entropia Universe'. https:// en.wikipedia.org/wiki/Entropia_Universe.

Williams, Maynard. 'Welcome to the Internet of Thinking'. *The Telegraph,* 8 May, 2018.

Wünsche, Burkhard and Stefan Marks, eds. *Conferences in Research and Practice in Information Technology,* vol.150. Sydney: Australian Computer Society, 2014.

Wycherley, Lynne. 'Electromagnetic Pollution Risks to Bees'. *The Beekeepers' Quarterly* 13, 2019, pp.54-57.

YouGov. *The Mobile Life Report 2006: How mobile phones change the way we live.* https:// iis.yougov.co.uk/extranets/ygarchives/content/pdf/CPW060101004_1.pdf.

Zaehner, R. C. *Hinduism.* New York: Oxford University Press, 1966.

Zuboff, Shoshana. *The Age of Surveillance Capitalism.* New York: Public Affairs, 2018.

—— Interview with John Naughton. ' "The Goal is to automate us": welcome to the age of surveillance capitalism'. *The Guardian,* 20 January, 2019.

INDEX

A note from the publisher

For more than a quarter of a century, **Temple Lodge Publishing** has made available new thought, ideas and research in the field of spiritual science.

Anthroposophy, as founded by Rudolf Steiner (1861-1925), is commonly known today through its practical applications, principally in education (Steiner-Waldorf schools) and agriculture (biodynamic food and wine). But behind this outer activity stands the core discipline of spiritual science, which continues to be developed and updated. True science can never be static and anthroposophy is living knowledge.

Our list features some of the best contemporary spiritual-scientific work available today, as well as introductory titles. So, visit us online at **www.templelodge.com** and join our emailing list for news on new titles.

If you feel like supporting our work, you can do so by buying our books or making a direct donation (we are a non-profit/ charitable organisation).

office@templelodge.com

TEMPLE LODGE

For the finest books of Science and Spirit